W9-BVE-788

HELP!
I'm not a
PERFECT
PARENT!

Overcoming
the Guilty-Parent
Syndrome

David R. Miller

ACCENT BOOKS
Denver, Colorado

ACCENT BOOKS
A division of Accent Publications
12100 West Sixth Avenue
P.O. Box 15337
Denver, Colorado 80215

Copyright © 1991 Accent Publications
Printed in the United States of America

All rights reserved. No portion of this book may be reproduced in any form without the written permission of the publishers, with the exception of brief excerpts in magazine reviews.

ISBN 0-89636-301-5

Library of Congress Catalog Card Number 90-85185

OVERTON MEMORIAL LIBRARY
HERITAGE CHRISTIAN UNIVERSITY
P.O. Box HCU
Florence, Alabama 35630

"I will behave myself wisely in a perfect way. O when wilt thou come unto me? I will walk within my house with a perfect heart."

Psalm 101:2

"Great is our Lord, and of great power: his understanding is infinite....The Lord taketh pleasure in them that fear him, in those that hope in his mercy....For he hath strengthened the bars of thy gates; he hath blessed thy children within thee."

Psalm 147:5,11,13

CONTENTS

1 / Diagnosing Parent Guilt

Kids! Who needs them?

You've probably heard that said more than once, usually from a parent trying to deal with some form of a child's misbehavior.

Others have said that parenting would be great—if it wasn't for those kids who keep confusing things.

And all too often these days, parents like you and me find ourselves faced with problems involving one of the kids who are threatening our own personal and spiritual stability with their misbehavior. We wonder if there is something wrong with our parenting efforts, and if there is anything we can do to remedy the situation.

This book is for parents who are in a confusing or difficult situation with a child. It's for parents struggling to raise a child or teenager in the nurture (love) and admonition (teaching) of the Lord. This book is for parents who love their children but who may be at a point where they do not like their children very much right now.

I must admit that I am a recovering guilty parent. Our last child is now almost grown, and we are *finally* seeing the fruits of our labors in the lives of our *grown* children. I know from my research and my own experience that guilt is a common feeling for all parents from time to time, and even more so for Christian parents because of the high standards we have for ourselves and the high expectations we have for our children.

This book isn't for kids or cowards. This book is for adults at some stage of parenting—future, present, or even past. This book is prayerfully designed to be both a "booster shot" of medication as well as a vaccination for the future child- or teen-based afflictions that beset most parents at some time. And it is for *today*, bringing to the surface the difficult issues of raising children for God in a godless world with trials and temptations that my parents and yours never had to face.

So, if you are ready to examine this issue of parent guilt, we will begin with something that happened to my family, an experience that brought me face to face with my own guilt as a Christian parent.

There we were, Linda and I, on our way to see Mr. Peters, our son's high school principal. The bad dream of every parent was happening to the Miller family. Though the drive was only about six miles, it seemed like an eternity before we arrived. No conversation in the car. No comments about the weather or traffic. Just deafening silence.

Linda knew when Karl Peters called that this was no little "late for class, talking in study hall" type problem. Karl was a family friend but was speaking with his "principal's voice." I guess only parents who have had such a call will know what I am talking about.

Honestly, I felt like *I* was in trouble, and I hadn't been in high school in twenty-five years! Pulling into the parking lot, walking down the hallway to Mr. Peters' office, I felt like a kid again. A kid in trouble.

Linda told me later that she felt the same guilt. You would have to know my wife to know how strange this sounded. Linda, unlike me, was *never* in trouble in school. A straight-A student, class officer, all the good stuff and none of the bad, that was Linda. But she felt guilty, too.

At least we didn't run into any of our friends who taught or worked at the school. We felt that just being there for that reason was tough enough without the added embarrassment of having to explain what was going on.

Boy, were we a picture of failure-based guilt! We each felt that we had let down not only our son, but also the school, the church, our friends...even the national debt felt more personal that day.

Karl was sensitive to our feelings and tried to make the best of this very difficult situation. He was a veteran of many of these meetings, of course. Wisely, he didn't try to small talk or console us; he got right to the reason for our being there.

Doug, our second child and only son, was being expelled for the rest of the semester. What our son did doesn't matter anymore. It wasn't a capital crime, but it was enough to require that we find another school for him to finish the eleventh grade. Though in doubt at the time, Doug did return to the school and graduated the following year with his class. I learned that in every graduating class some parents are much more thankful for the miracle of high school graduation than others might be.

Doug got over this episode pretty quickly—too quickly to suit his mother and me—but the aftershock stayed with Linda and me for quite a long time. In reflecting on the event and our feelings, I couldn't get over how embarrassed and guilty, ashamed really, I felt. I felt like it was *my* fault that my sixteen-year-old son had chosen to do a stupid and careless thing. I felt like *I* should be embarrassed, as if *I* had done something wrong.

How in the world did this incredible "blame shift" occur? What had happened to Linda and me, and mostly to me, to cause such feelings of guilt? And what continued to bother me was what would happen if Doug or one of the other kids would get into trouble at some future time? Is this what people mean when they talk about being "parents forever"?

Was I wrong in feeling embarrassed and guilty? Was I wrong to allow these feelings to weigh so heavily on me? Was this parental guilt a Christian thing to experience? And if not, what could I do to relieve those negative feelings so that I could be both a better father for my children and a better Christian, too?

What follows is what I learned about myself, my own upbringing, the teachings of the various pastors I have listened to through the years, my thoughts, meditations, and prayers, and the answers I found.

Did I find answers?

Yes. I found answers that turned my life around as a Christian and as a parent. I found answers that made me feel, for the first time in my life and ministry, that I was beginning to understand what I needed to understand about guilt, shame, and embarrassment in Christian parenting. What you will read in the following pages is part my own story, my recovery from parental guilt, and part the stories that hundreds of Christian families have shared with me in the years I have been a family counselor. Just as I diagnosed my own level of parental guilt, I will invite you to do the same. The process is largely painless and very private. No deep psychoanalytical investigations will occur, and the results may be as liberating for you as they were and are for me. Join me in assessing your level of parental guilt.

Diagnosing Parental Guilt

Think about how you behave when the subject of your children comes up in conversation.

Do you smile when you reflect on the experience of being a parent?

What kinds of feelings do you experience when your kids pester, disobey, talk back, and generally become obnoxious in your presence?

Can you accept the reality that sometimes you dislike your children because of their behavior even though your love for them remains unchanged?

These are important questions for parents.

I work almost exclusively with the parents of children and adolescents. For the most part, these families are conservative, Christian, intact, non-abusive, but they are still being called on to understand and deal with temporarily misbehaving youngsters.

However, I have found that the misbehavior is not the worst obstacle parents face in helping their kids; it's the manner in which the parents handle the negatives, including their temporary negative feelings about their children. If such feelings are not recognized and dealt with appropriately, parents are vulnerable to what I call the guilty-parent syndrome.

I have found that many parents are *not* dealing with their negative feelings very well. Evidence for this can be seen in the counselor's office of elementary, junior high, and high schools, and in reports by parents and their children. Causes for the guilty-parent syndrome include the parent's attitudes, values, and family history, of course, but also responsible are the trends evident in our society moving us toward secular humanism and away from traditional Judeo-Christian values. Christian parents bear much of the negative brunt of this trend through messages in the public schools and in the secular media which emphasize children's rights

11

and the importance of self over family and others.

Christian parents are constantly being told that there is a better way to rear children, but the "better way" is often nothing more than a permissive chaos cloaked in a thin disguise called "new age parenting." Restraint and discipline, we are told, will likely stunt our children's growth and maturity and turn them into nothing more than well-dressed, carefully clipped robots. We are encouraged to allow our kids to make important decisions before they are ready and to bail them out when it comes time to pay the price for their behavior.

And if we don't "bend to the trend," guilt is thrust upon us because we are trying to apply biblical teachings and values to "new age" problems.

But what's worse is that many of us have accepted that guilt. Many Christian parents have bought the story being sold by the media and are deep in the throes of self-doubt and guilt.

The media bombards families with plastic-lipped, smiling actors who have no family problems that cannot be solved in a half-hour or sixty-minute television program. The important issues of childrearing always conform to the program's format and are dealt with by abundant quips, jokes, happy teasing, and a big hug just before the commercial.

"Why," Christian parents ask, "can't we be as easygoing as Heathcliff and Clair Huxtable on *The Cosby Show*?"

"Why can't we be as all-knowing and tolerant as the Keatons on *Family Ties* or the Seavers on *Growing Pains*?"

No matter how unrealistic such television shows may be, they impart a powerful message that we *ought* to be like them, and if we aren't, we *should* feel guilty.

Diagnosing our individual level of parental guilt is one important step all Christian parents can take as we learn how to resist the pressure to go along with the world's way of parenting and follow biblical teaching.

So, if you are willing, take the 15-question quiz that follows. Simply answer "yes" or "no" to each question, and then we will score your test.

GUILTY PARENT QUIZ

1. Have you read three or more books on childrearing during the last twelve months?   Y___ N___

2. Are you uncomfortable or worried about taking your child or adolescent to visit family or friends?

     Y___ N___

3. Have you spoken with your pastor recently about your child or adolescent?   Y___ N___

4. Do you find yourself questioning your own judgment when you spank or otherwise discipline your youngster?   Y___ N___

5. When the phone rings unexpectedly, are you flooded by negative or troubling thoughts about your child or adolescent?   Y___ N___

6. Are your parents divorced?   Y___ N___

7. Are your spouse's parents divorced? Y___ N___

8. Are you often concerned about your child or adolescent as you fall asleep at night or as you wake up in the morning?   Y___ N___

9. Do you often wonder if you are a good parent?

     Y___ N___

10. Have you discussed a problem your child or adolescent may be having with a friend recently?

     Y___ N___

11. Have you been to school about your child or adolescent this school year? Y___ N___

12. Do you feel like apologizing after administering discipline? Y___ N___

13. Do you feel less in control as a parent now than when your child was an infant? Y___ N___

14. Have you had two or more serious disagreements with your spouse about child-rearing this year?

Y___ N___

15. When you discuss children or parenting with friends or family, do you feel uncomfortable and hope the subject will change? Y___ N___

The more "yes" responses, the greater the likelihood that parental guilt is present. Eight or more "yes" responses are reason for concern and self-evaluation, and twelve or more "yes" responses indicate that guilt is a negative reality in the family and help should be sought.

A good place to start looking for help and answers is in the family dynamics.

First of all, a syndrome is a set of symptoms, not just one or two. A syndrome is a series of behaviors, thoughts, or emotions which affect the way we analyze a situation and react to certain circumstances. As we share the following eight possible symptoms and sources of parental guilt, I want you to reflect on your own experiences as a child and adolescent for insights on the reason for the guilt you may be feeling today.

Child-Bound Anxiety

Anxiety, the first symptom, is usually defined as an intensely uncomfortable feeling of uneasiness or uncertainty.

Actually, anxiety is a pain manifestation that most people seek to avoid or relieve.

Anxiety comes in two forms, free-floating and bound. Of the two, free-floating anxiety is much the more difficult to treat because the root of the problem, the anxiety, "floats" from one person, object, place, or event to another in an unpredictable and often unexplainable way.

Bound anxiety is quite different because the source of the anxiety is known and tends to be consistent and predictable. Bound anxiety tends to be "bound" to one child or one type of situation, for example, illness or disobedience, and it is more easily controlled.

Free-floating anxiety in Christian parents tends to rise out of our own experiences as children and usually takes considerable effort and professional intervention by a Christian counselor or psychologist to be brought under control. Bound anxiety is more easily treated for the reasons mentioned above.

Child-bound anxiety occurs when some important percentage of a parent's self-concept is "invested" in a child. My perception of my performance and value as a parent depends on the behavior of my child or adolescent. And, of course, since my child or adolescent will fail at some point (he or she is only human after all), when that failure occurs, my anxiety level is likely to go through the roof.

Why? Anxiety rises to meet the level of expectations imposed on us *by our parents when we were children.* Our anxiety level, therefore, is dictated by the expectations our parents had of us as children and have simply become "transgenerational" as they moved from us as parents to our children.

This anxiety naturally leads to intense feelings of guilt. And most parents inevitably accept partial or complete responsibility for the misbehavior of a child or teen. The guilt can be fostered by one specific child, event, or by anything associated with parenting. Unfortunately, parents usually lack the resources to deal with the anxiety and resultant guilt. So the guilty feelings create anxiety, the anxiety makes us feel guilty for feeling anxious (after all, we are Christians aren't we?), and then we feel guilty both as parents *and* as Christians.

What a vicious cycle!

Parents who experience undefined anxiety when they think or talk about their child or teen easily "progress" into a full-blown guilty-parent syndrome. If we can't explain the anxiety we feel, if we are unable to explain why our teenager or child continues to misbehave, we will assume that it *must* be something we have done. It just *must* be out fault. This may seem extreme or irrational at first glance, but such feelings are very common in Christian parents.

Overly Strict or Lax Discipline

Another symptom of the guilty-parent syndrome is found in the extremes of overly strict discipline or very lax and careless discipline. Balance is the key in virtually every aspect of good parenting. Remember Paul's admonition to the Philippians? "Let your moderation be known unto all men" (4:5). It applies in parenting, too. These extremes of too much or too little discipline reflect either an over-reaction by parents or inconsistency brought on by parental guilt following discipline.

Some parents who experience the guilty-parent syndrome seek a solution in tougher disciplinary procedures. But excessively harsh discipline has many serious "side effects" such as emotional reactions in the child or teenager of anger, bitterness, resentment, and perhaps most importantly, a tendency toward violence. Parents want to consider carefully the *real* message being sent by harsh methods and prayerfully consider Paul's words in Ephesians 6:4, "And, ye fathers, provoke not your children to wrath: but bring them up in the nurture and admonition of the Lord."

Other parents, because of the way they were disciplined as children, deal with their guilt and insecurity by becoming too lax and lenient in their God-given responsibilities as parents. The difference between leniency and flexibility is very important. Leniency means inconsistency in most cases. Leniency tells the youngster, "I know you did it and you deserve to be punished, but I will let you get away with it this time." In this case, leniency becomes the "leaven" mentioned in I Corinthians 5:6 and, just as a little leaven (sin) leavens the whole lump, leniency teaches that some sins are minor and okay to be overlooked. The child will naturally take this as permission to do the wrongful act again.

But flexibility carries the message of I Samuel 16:7 in which we are reminded that, "The Lord seeth not as man seeth; for man looketh on the outward appearance, but the Lord looketh on the heart." Flexibility is "looking on the heart" of a child or teenager and giving parental consideration to age, emotional state, circumstances, peer pressure, and other variables and, after careful consideration, telling that young person that we understand how such a thing might have happened, and we will trust them not to make the same mistake again.

Overly strict or extreme discipline is usually the result of parental love that has been translated into a need to control. If parents feel guilty about being less than perfect in their own lives, sometimes they attempt to reassure themselves by becoming authoritarian and strict.

Experience shows that we also attempt to control that which most frightens us. If we feel incompetent as parents, we will tend to "toughen up" in order to prove to ourselves that we are better parents than we feel we really are.

For example, in an effort to keep children safe and protected at any cost, parents may choose to demonstrate their love for the children by forcing them into a position where they can do nothing but obey. The truism of obedience being more important than sacrifice (worship) becomes a parenting philosophy. How many children have been raised knowing very well that to obey is the *best* thing a child can do and that a spanking is more to be desired than the fat of rams (I Samuel 15:22)?

If anyone was helped by severe discipline, we might be able to find some virtue in it. But overly strict parents will remain unsure of themselves as parents, and their guilt will only increase. The concept of "beating the devil out of a child" is not the teaching of Christ and leads to major problems when a parent comes face to face with a problem that will *not* be cured with toughness. Unfortunately, this leads some into the dark valley of child abuse, a reality confirmed in recent years by an ever greater acquaintance between conservative Christian families and Child Protective Services.

On the other hand, lax discipline produces different results even though the cause is the same. Parents who question their own abilities may try to earn the child's obedience and respect through bribes and rewards. Even though children and teens prefer laxity over harshness, the lesson that Mom and Dad are not really in charge around here becomes firmly established.

Each form of inadequate discipline, harsh or lax, communicates some very important messages to any child or teenager. Either he will believe that Mom and Dad don't care enough about him to accept the hassle of confronting his behaviors, or he feels that Mom and Dad simply don't know *how* to discipline him effectively.

Maybe both!

Either extreme to discipline makes the kids think, "If they loved me, they wouldn't let me do things that are bad for me. They'd care where I am and what I am doing. They'd care who my friends are. They wouldn't be afraid to tell me 'no'."

Parenting is a long road to travel covering many years and

lots of territory. Mom and Dad must drive straight down that road, staying as close to the middle as possible even though a child or teenager may be weaving from side to side, falling or nearly falling into the sin-dug ditches on either side. Mom and Dad must stay the course and be their centerline for life. As Paul encouraged the Philippian church: "Holding forth the word of life; that I may rejoice in the day of Christ, that I have not run in vain, neither laboured in vain" (Philippians 2:16).

Compulsive Book Reading

All cf us tend to seek out "experts" when we hit one of the brick walls of parenting. If we find ourselves shopping for "answer" books, tuning into experts on television or radio, and looking for seminars to attend, we may have a problem of parent guilt. As one who leads parenting seminars around the country, I don't want to diminish the contribution such educational resources can make to parenting, but *needing* such resources is one sign among many that guilt is the motivating force.

What we need to address is *why* we are seeking answers. There is a normal desire in all good parents to want to be as expert as we can be in our parenting. Personally, I read an average of a book a week, most of which relate in some way to the family. *Wanting* to know is one thing. *Needing* to know is another! The compulsive drive to attend any seminar that comes to town, buy every new book that comes out, and become reliant on what others say about the family reflects parental self-doubt based on feelings of guilt. Others do *not* know our children as well as we do.

Advice, yes. Insight, yes. Slavish acceptance, no. Discernment is the key to the information we gather.

Networking

Networking is an attempt to get as much help, as much

19

expertise, as much input into a situation as possible. Controlled and carefully thought-out networking is a legitimate method of problem-solving that can be useful.

But when parents begin networking, it is often a sign that we are seeking affirmation of our methods rather than new information. What networking often amounts to is a simple vote-gathering contest on whether or not we are doing the right thing. This is similar to the elementary-age child who cannot follow any direction in the classroom without first coming up to the teacher's desk and asking, "Is this what you meant? Is this how I should do it? Is this okay?"

Parents normally do not need very much affirmation that they are doing the right thing. Looking for constant affirmation reflects parental insecurity based on feelings of guilt. If parents seek information for its own sake, there is no problem. In fact, we should all try to be as informed as possible. But information and affirmation are not the same and reflect far different motivations. Needing to have our parenting methods affirmed by others reflects the guilty-parent syndrome.

A Harvest of Secrets

We all have secrets and that's all right. Some things should only be discussed with God. But the tendency to keep quiet normally doesn't apply to parents. We like to brag about our kids, tend to magnify their good points, and minimize their bad points.

But, when we find ourselves keeping certain kinds of truth "under wraps" or harboring suspicions about our youngsters, a red flag of warning should go up.

If we are uncomfortable or embarrassed when asked about our children, we should stop and consider the source of such feelings. There were times when I had such feelings. There were times when Linda and I didn't want *anyone* to know about the struggles we were having as parents. And there were things I didn't want to hear about or learn about because it might reflect on my ability as a parent, thus making me feel guilty.

A compulsion to hide things about our offspring reflects a certain degree of insecurity about parental competence. Staying within the boundaries of normal family privacy and honoring commitments of confidentiality is normal. The extreme desire to keep others from finding out what's going on in the family is another symptom of the guilty-parent syndrome.

Husband/Wife Conflict

Someone once said that if a husband and wife always agree, one of them is unnecessary! We might have to look a long time to find biblical support for this saying, but the reality of this present age (and probably all past ages) is that husbands and wives do not agree on all matters affecting the family.

And when it comes to children, parents are supposed to disagree, but within certain parameters of love, good sense, and putting the welfare of the other above one's own (Philippians 2:3).

I can relate to this idea personally. The most serious arguments Linda and I have had in thirty years of marriage have focused on the children. Much of the reason for this was found in our own family backgrounds and our professions. We each had good parents, and we are both university professors as well as parents.

But in spite of these advantages, we each brought to our parenting our own ideas, which usually concurred—but not always. Our uncertainty as parents was directly related to our age at the time and the interest we had in maintaining a good "testimony" through our children. I will say more about this later, but for now let me emphasize that *continuing* disagreements over the children reflect a deeper problem. It may be that each parent is failing to trust the judgment of the other. Or it may reflect vastly different family influences or education. The disagreements may be based on the unwillingness of one parent to follow biblical principles or allow the Holy Spirit to lead in an uncertain direction.

Constant bickering, whatever the reason, should not be overlooked. It is a warning signal that something *is* wrong between the parents, and it needs to be corrected before permanent damage occurs.

Sleeplessness

Insomnia may seem out of place in this discussion, but I can assure you from personal and counseling experience that sleeplessness belongs right here. I know that the inability to sleep is a key symptom of the guilty-parent syndrome.

Linda and I experienced chronic insomnia the summer between our son's seventeenth and eighteenth birthdays. Looking back on it, we usually refer to that time as the "sleepless summer of seventeen." That summer Doug decided to assert his independence and resist the established curfew. Somehow he reasoned that as long as school was out for the summer and his work hours were limited to afternoons, he shouldn't have to come in at any special time, especially as long as he stayed out of trouble.

We went round and round about that curfew. Doug continued to try to assert his independence by coming in when he pleased while we (mostly me) waited up for him, prepared for yet another battle as soon as he walked through the door. We finally reached a partially satisfying agreement even though neither Linda nor I, nor Doug for that matter, got what we wanted. But during that summer there was a definite shortage of peace, tranquility, and sleep at the Miller residence.

What we learned from this experience was that sometimes, with some young people, certain confrontations are bound to happen no matter what. Doug's insistence on determining his own hours reflected his personality and the parenting he had received from us. Perhaps we taught him to stand up for what he believed was right, and looking back on it, I think I prefer Doug the way he was that summer to a totally compliant, never complain, never-become-independent-from-parents type of adolescent. We learned that some kids simply have to work through some issues if they are going to grow up. And while we certainly didn't like it at the time, it probably had to happen.

Confusion

A final symptom of the guilty-parent syndrome is parental confusion. In this context we are talking about the parent's inability to understand child or adolescent misbehavior as well as failing to find correct answers for such misbehavior.

As parents we need to recognize this frustration and deal with it. The reason for the behavior is the most troubling aspect, though.

"Why is she doing this weird stuff?" we ask ourselves. "Surely purple hair and safety pin earrings can't really be that popular with the kids." But they are popular and will continue to be so as long as we let it get to us. It's a fact that *some* of our young people will do virtually *anything* if it upsets adults, and especially authority figures like parents and teachers.

The second kind of parental confusion is more directly tied to a specific behavior or set of behaviors. We ask ourselves: "Why can't Tim be better at algebra?" Or we ask ourselves why Sue or Jeremy insist on associating with all the "wrong" kids at school.

We seek specific answers to specific problems, and when the answers escape us, we feel like failures, and we become shamefaced in front of our friends. We just don't realize how many families are going through the same kinds of developmental difficulties with *their* kids as we are with ours.

Most of us only find this out when our kids are grown and we no longer feel guilty or responsible when they make bad decisions or stumble morally.

Remember that a syndrome is a *set* of symptoms. We have to expect that our kids will experience some difficulties in growing up, and we, their parents, are likely to feel guilty and responsible for those problems. When we see ourselves manifesting some or all of the symptoms discussed so far, it's time to get help.

Feeling guilty is a terrible experience. Feeling guilty without knowing why is much worse. The feelings we experience usually grow out of the intense love and care we have for our children; often it comes when we have tried our hardest to do what we believe is best. Then we look around and see that many good families have trouble raising children and teenagers in this corrupt world. And we look a little farther and we see parents who really *are* doing a bad job of parenting but who don't seem to be as unhappy or worried as we. Parent guilt can be a real mystery.

But before we dig ourselves deeper into that guilt trap, we need to remember that God has an answer for every problem our kids can throw at us. Parents plus God make a majority in every decision, and if we can overcome our very human tendency to accept guilt and responsibility for the errors of our young people, we will be able to rejoice one day and repeat from our heart the proverb that says, "The father of the righteous shall greatly rejoice, and he that begetteth a wise child shall have joy of him. Thy father and thy mother shall be glad, and she that bare thee shall rejoice" (Proverbs 23:24-25).

Points for Parents to Ponder

These questions at the end of each chapter are simply to encourage careful thought and reflection. The questions are phrased in such a way that every "yes" answer indicates a tendency to accept the kind of parental guilt we have been discussing. These are informal and should not be taken as an absolute indication that guilt is present since other circumstances might explain a "yes" answer. However, as a working counselor, I recommend that if "yes" answers are frequent, you may want to find a Christian counselor with whom to talk.

1. Do you often feel as if you are losing your personal identity and are becoming submerged in your children?

2. Do you find yourself making excuses for the behavior of your children or teenagers?

3. Can you identify with the experiences of Linda and me when we were in Mr. Peters' office?

4. Do you sometimes feel that you are disappointing others when your young person misbehaves?

5. Are you uncomfortable when friends or family ask about your children?

6. Do you feel as though your pastor or others are blaming you for the misbehavior, no matter how minor, of your children?

7. Did you answer "yes" to a majority of the questions on the "Guilty Parent Quiz"?

8. Can you identify with the concept of "bound anxiety" explained in this chapter?

9. Would you characterize your discipline procedures as very lax or very strict?

10. Do you feel that your children or teenagers are presently creating problems for you as a parent?

2 / The Roots of Parental Guilt

The Smith family is a real family. Names have been changed to protect the innocent, of course, but their story might help us get started on the trail of the elusive roots of parental guilt.

Like myself, Fred Smith is impatient to a fault. Nothing bothers fathers like us more than arriving late to *anything*, especially a church service. But that is what is facing Fred as he waits impatiently for his tribe to file out of the house and into the car.

Sensing their father's unhappiness with their slow preparation for leaving, seven-year-old Billy and nine-year-old Ray race for their favorite spots in the back seat, scaring their fourteen-year-old sister Rachel with the possibility of a sticky handprint on her white skirt, the one she *knows* will attract the attention of a certain boy at church. Four-year-old Sally and Mom are the last to pile into the car, Mom apologizing and Sally oblivious to Dad's impatience.

And then the boys start to disagree, shout, and push each

27

other, bringing pleas for help from Rachel, still worried about her white skirt. Fred, like countless other harried fathers, responds to their shouts by shouting at them to sit still and be quiet or face the consequences later. The boys know that Dad will carry out his threat, and so they settle down for the brief ride to church.

As they exit the car, Dad stops to offer one last word of "encouragement" to the boys. "One word, one poke or punch in church, and you two will wish you were born into a family on Mars. Got it?"

"Yes, sir," the boys reply, knowing that Dad is serious this time.

Rachel has reserved her best smile for right now.

"Dad," she says with the tone of voice unique to a teenager about to ask for something, "can I *please* sit with Julie and the other kids? *Please?*"

Reluctantly, Fred agrees, but insists that they sit where they can be seen.

All Sally wants to do right now is lean on her dad's arm and get the coloring book ready for later.

All is well with the world. The service is great. The kids are, well, okay! And on the way out of the church Fred and his wife Donna even receive a compliment on their well-behaved children. Fred puts on his humble face while the man is talking, but Donna can't help smiling. *If he only knew what punishment awaited these kids at home if they misbehaved,* she thinks.

But, there's no point in spoiling her husband's momentary pride in his parenting skills. She would bring him down to earth later on with some homework papers that needed to be signed for Monday morning at school.

What Fred has just gone through has been experienced by most Christian parents at one time or another. Raising smaller children in an obedient and disciplined fashion takes *will* rather than *skill*. Skill becomes much more important with teenagers like Rachel.

Rachel is actually a good example for this discussion. Rachel knew that if she wanted to obtain permission to sit with Julie, her "pre-request" behavior had to be exemplary. And it was. And she got permission. Rachel had learned how to live in her family and how to deal with the personality characteristics of her parents. Rachel was becoming a skilled teenager.

Fred and Donna, Linda and I, and you and your spouse either have learned or will learn that just about anyone who wants to control the behavior of *young* children can do so. Little kids live in a land of giants, after all, and they learn very early on that their very survival depends on keeping Mom and Dad happy, at least most of the time. We parents sometimes forget how well our children learn that they are dependent on us for *everything* and that we are supposed to use that dependence as a tool to help them learn what they need to learn about life.

But adolescents are another class of beings altogether. Rachel, like most teenagers, was able to control her behavior at home and church so that she could get something she wanted. Of course, this is not the only reason young people behave, but it serves to illustrate the interactional nature of dealing with teenagers. Teenagers, unlike children, behave themselves *only* because they want to, and it falls to parents of teens to find ways to encourage them to want to do the right thing.

It is not so much "making" teens behave as encouraging them to "want" to behave. It is choices we are talking about here, not physical force or psychological coercion. Giving teens choices is treating them like the young adult human beings (not old children) they really are.

And negotiation!

When we learn how to negotiate with our teenagers without compromising important principles, more than

29

half the battle is won.

But before we look at negotiation, let's face a few facts. Teenagers *are* going to act crazy at times. There are several reasons for this "temporary insanity" including hormone production and release, peer pressure, the new ability to think like an adult, and many others. Maybe junk food explains part of it! One thing is for sure. There are as many reasons for, and varieties of, adolescent craziness as there are adolescents.

Having a temporarily insane teenager in your home is not a disgrace anymore than Dad losing his hair or Mom getting some wrinkles is a disgrace. Some degree of adolescent silliness and unpredictability is as natural a part of human development as the changes that afflict middle-age parents.

But when a problem magnifies and explodes into a crisis of major proportions, we have to deal with it in as serious a manner as needed. It is not the problem that should embarrass parents, but the all too common refusal to deal with the problem.

Although I generally recommend against judging other parents, it is important that we parents judge ourselves. We must evaluate our actions and reactions, our motives and goals, and see if we have the mind of Christ in what we are doing or whether we are acting on human impulses alone. We must be able to step back and objectively look at what we have been doing and the results our actions have produced. If we cannot do this, we are vulnerable to becoming neglectful, careless parents. Self-evaluation, call it self-judgment if you wish, is critical in understanding the dynamics of parental guilt.

Irrational Beliefs of Parents

The roots of parental guilt lie buried in the expectations we have for ourselves as parents. Are our expectations for ourselves reasonable? Are they rational? Do they make sense

30

when compared to God's Word? Or have we set unobtainable goals for ourselves and our children?

Let me point out something about parenting that may seem out of context at first glance. How many *specific* examples of good *or* bad parenting can you find in the Bible? If you answered "none," I think you are on the right track.

We are given very little, if any, specific advice on how to discipline children and what kind of love and discipline will get the best results with our children.

Of course, there are many examples of good and bad *people* in the Bible. We know about Lot's wicked *adult* daughters (Genesis 19:14, 30-38) and about Eli's reprobate *adult* sons (I Samuel 2:12, 22-25). We even know that Eli spoiled his sons as adults, but we are not told what happened when they were children. We know that Samuel's *adult* sons took bribes and perverted justice (I Samuel 8:1-3), but we do not know what kind of father Samuel was as they were growing up. We know that the *adult* Absalom, the favorite son of King David, rebelled and coveted his father's throne, but we are not told why or how he grew up into the adult he became (II Samuel 15).

Again and again we are warned of the fruits of adult rebellion but we are never told what, if anything, specifically brought these people to their fates. We are told what King David did wrong with Bathsheba, but God doesn't share with us David's behavior as a parent or his parents' behavior with him.

We know that Moses, Aaron, Abraham, and other patriarchs of the Bible were family men, and sometimes we are told of their general character and how they behaved as husbands. Abraham is a good example of this. But nothing of substance is reported regarding their behavior as fathers. Similarly with mothers, we are sometimes told that Sarah and other wives and mothers loved and cared for their children, but we have no idea who did the disciplining, who

31

was strict and who was lenient, who spanked and who didn't.

The New Testament as well lets us know that many of the disciples were husbands and fathers, but nothing is revealed concerning their performance as family leaders. Jesus Himself gives no specific teaching about how to deal with child or adolescent misbehavior.

This is not a criticism of the Bible. I do not wish to be struck with lightning! I believe there is a very good reason for these apparent omissions. We know that God laid down certain principles for dealing with people, including young people and children. We are to do all that we do in love (Philippians 2:2-3), for example. This broad and very important principle applies as much to the roles of mother and father as it does to Christian growth. Whatever we do with our children, we are to do out of a heart of love.

Therefore, principles such as love and esteeming others higher than oneself provide us with a biblical approach to childrearing. Should we discipline? If so, do it in love! Should we instruct? If so, do it in love. Should we seek justice? Only in love. Whatever we do as parents is to be done out of a heart ruled and controlled by love for the child. This principle alone would eliminate all child abuse, all neglect, all child exploitation in its many forms. Everything that could be harmful to a child could be prevented if parents and other adults functioned exclusively out of a heart of love.

I believe the Holy Spirit did not direct the human authors of Scripture to share specific parenting practices of the heroes of the faith because God knew we humans would make idols out of those historical techniques, and God knows that what worked in Bible days may not work as well in the world of each today since then. God knows that our children have unique and individual qualities entrusted to *us*, their parents to discern. General principles set down by God are designed to protect our children from parents who would follow the letter of the law rather than the heart of God for their children.

There may be more to say about this important topic later on, but for now let's take a look at some irrational beliefs common to Christian parents and see what we can do about them.

Irrational Belief #1: **Parents should be able to control the behavior of their child or adolescent.**
Someone made the observation, "Children are people, too." Most of us gradually realize the truth of this statement as we watch our children grow. The fact that children and adolescents are people should impress all parents with the fact that those independent human beings will do what they *want* to do. The challenge is to bring young people to the point where they *want* to do the right things, Christ-honoring things, in life.

Parents who set a standard for themselves that *their* children or teens will not misbehave are to be admired for their optimism. But this goal is and always has been impossible to obtain. Something very strange happens to us when our kids become more than toddlers and begin to assert their God-given need for independence and personhood. And when they become teenagers! We all have to find out rather abruptly that we must work *with*, rather than *on,* our young people to guide their attitudes and behavior in a direction that will please God, them, and us.

Plan on it right now, our children and teenagers *will* misbehave. They will do so because they are human and are sin-influenced (just like their parents!), and they will misbehave because they have been raised by us! Love them as we will, we are not *perfect* role models and they will not be perfect either.

Of course they will misbehave, but as long as they learn from their actions (and we do, too!), God is honored.

Perhaps we parents should hedge a little bit on claiming complete control over our children and teenagers. Influence

33

and direction are more effective if our expectations are reasonable, and we will have more input into the thoughts and behavior of our youngsters if we are perceived by them as reasonable parents.

The real conflict arises because we must confront ourselves when our young people ignore our advice or make an active choice to go in another direction. Parents can be sure of one thing—we will be faced with this dilemma at some time or other. If we insist on taking personal responsibility for the choices other people make, even if those people are our children, we are virtually doomed to feelings of failure when those decisions turn out to be unwise. Parents cannot overcome the guilty-parent syndrome unless and until we stop accepting responsibility for the behavior of others.

However, we can win if we develop a mindset which acknowledges that God has a plan for each child. The next step is to recognize that God's plan may not agree with *our* plan for our kids. There may be a point in life when your child chooses to leave the family and marry someone not totally of your liking. Hard as it may be to accept, there is *no* biblical requirement that the parents be in agreement with the choice of a marriage partner. Once our children have accepted the Lord as personal Savior, they have as much of the Holy Spirit residing in them as we do in us. At some point, all parents must let go and let God!

Irrational Belief #2: **Parents who avoid making serious mistakes in parenting will have children free of major problems.**

"What did we do wrong?"

This is the lament of parents who expect their behavior to be the controlling factor in their children's behavior. It is probably the most natural thing in the world to look for flaws in our childrearing practices in order to explain the unacceptable behavior of a child or teenager. It is usually much easier for parents to accept blame for such misbehavior than to admit that their child or teen is capable of sinful behavior on his own. This irrational belief tends to produce parents who are legalistically self-controlled and conformist in their own lives. But this "good" behavior doesn't come so much from a desire to please God as from the mistaken belief that parents are and should be capable of controlling every aspect of child or teen behavior. "My children will do as they see me doing" is the often heard comment from legalistically oriented Christian parents. This notion is usually coupled with a more secret fear that, "God will get me (embarrass me) through my children if I don't behave myself."

Parents who hold this position tend to experience a life filled with neurotic self-doubt because they have placed an artificial standard on themselves, one that is impossible to attain. No parent is good enough or powerful enough to be able to bribe God into giving them good children. Furthermore, God doesn't need parents to be perfect in order for Him to love them. God loves us and our children regardless of our mistakes or the mistakes of our children. Only God is truly capable of genuinely unconditional love.

Irrational Belief #3: **Parents are only worthwhile if their children grow up to be Christians.**

Linda and I have three grown children. From our experiences as Christians and parents, and my experiences as a family counselor, we know how serious the issue of personal salvation really is. Often a child is pushed in the direction of making a premature decision for Christ by parents who care more for their own peace of mind than for the ability of the child to understand. Nothing is more normal than wanting a child to become the best person he can be, and for Christian parents, being the best means being the best *Christian.* But let me ask you to consider some very important questions about children and salvation.

Is there anything a parent can do to guarantee the salvation of their children?

The first impulse many of us would have is to say, "Yes, of course there is."

This is usually followed by a listing of the things we can do to encourage a salvation decision.

1. Witness to them.
2. Take them to church.
3. Expose them to the gospel.
4. Ask them leading questions about salvation at various times in their development.
5. Ask the Sunday School teacher to teach lessons on salvation.
6. Arrange for a pastoral visit at the right time.
7. Pray for their salvation.

And the list goes on and on.

But the question remains. Is there anything a parent or anyone else can do to *assure* the salvation of a child or anyone else?

There can be only one answer: No.

To follow our parental impulse and say "yes" is to put ourselves on an equal level with God. This answer would reduce the death, burial, and resurrection of Jesus Christ to nothing but a symbol. No one "gets" children saved! That is the work of the Holy Spirit and only the Holy Spirit. Romans 11:6 says, "And if by grace, then is it no more of works (even parents' works): otherwise grace is no more grace. But if it be of works, then is it no more grace: otherwise work is no more work."

When I counseled a couple about a disobedient and rebellious teenager last year, this irrational and unbiblical belief surfaced. After we had explored at length each relevant passage of Scripture, I asked how they felt about what we were reading in the Bible.

After a pause, the father responded, "Well, it *ought* to be in the Bible!"

I share this father's feelings. But each of us must come to grips with the basic truth that God has no grandchildren. Each human being must make his or her own choice about salvation. As difficult as this may be to internalize, we must accept the fact that when God grants us the responsibility of raising *His* children, we also accept the potential heartache of seeing a child choose to follow a path away from salvation. For those who believe God's Word, there is simply no way around this basic truth.

We are not without influence. We certainly are not helpless in the battle for the souls of our children. Even though the basic truth of individual decision remains, we still have the awesome and powerful ability to pray for and set the best example we can for our kids. What God expects is that we make it as easy as possible for our kids to choose Christ's sacrifice for their redemption.

We pray. We wait. We witness. And ultimately we understand that we cannot do the work of the Holy Spirit in the life of any other person, even our own children. Nothing will put us on our knees like rearing children!

Irrational Belief #4: **If Christian parents are to be happy and content, our children must never get into serious trouble; they must be on every honor role at school; they must graduate from college, and they must have a perfect marriage.**

What a mouthful!

If it is unreasonable for parents to expect to be in control of our child's ultimate relationship with God, it is also unreason-able that we allow our happiness and contentment as Christian adults to be controlled by our children. God has a specific relationship in mind for parents and children, and it is a one-way relationship pointing to God.

Let me lay a little more groundwork for this. It is often said that children are gifts from God, little bundles of joy predestined to be the delight of their parents' existence. I wonder how many of us have considered the opposite possibility: That we parents may be gifts to our children rather than they to us!

Think with me for a moment. By the time most adults have children, we have been on this earth for twenty or more years developing a personality, a set of values, individual character traits, an education, and much more. We marry another individual with the same developmental track. Then God adds a child to the family.

Now if you were God, would you have prepared a child to meet the needs, personality, etc. of the adults waiting down there on earth or would you have prepared *in advance* the parents on earth who would be best able to meet the needs of this new child? In other words, doesn't it make more sense to see ourselves as parents being gifts from God to our children rather than the other way around?

Each child comes into this life with a special set of built-in abilities and limitations. The child is helpless, almost the most helpless of all God's creations at birth. Without the parents (or another caretaker), the child will die. And God has prepared us to meet the needs of our children. The giving goes from parents to children, never children to parents.

Parents who expect to be the providers for their children will never be disappointed. Parents who expect their children to provide for them and meet their needs will *always* be disappointed.

Why?

Parents with a newborn normally lavish love and attention on their little lump of fat and wrinkles. We dote on the baby, show him or her off to anyone who will take a look, and we make plans for the presidency or the National Football

League. The baby will smile and coo once in a while, and that's usually enough to make parents happy.

But sometimes things go wrong!

Sometimes parents, often mothers, get their priorities mixed up, and they begin meeting their own needs for love, attention, commitment, and reason for living in the child. The child has then become a parent, a provider instead of a recipient as God had intended. When we say or behave in ways that indicate that our happiness depends on the behavior of our children, we have reversed God's order for the family.

To believe that parents can only be happy and content as long as their children measure up to parental expectations is to be disobedient to God's teachings on the family.

Children and adolescents, even grown children, can be given control of their parent's lives through this priority reversal. Families in which child abuse, sexual abuse and incest, or "smother love" exist are always families where the children are perceived as existing for the use and enjoyment of their parents. God help us to avoid doing this!

As long as we keep our giving/receiving relationship with our children in the proper direction and in the proper balance, the joy inherent in family living will be nurtured.

I'm sure you could add to this list from your experiences as a parent. And whatever our irrational expectancies may be, they are grounded in our love for our children and our desire to be the best parents we can be. I believe that once we have placed ourselves in the proper relationship with God, we will have a better understanding of what He expects from us as parents.

When we accept the realities of genuine Christian parenting, we can more easily relax, serve God in the proper spirit, and enjoy the children He has loaned to us. These realities, once again...

1. God is in charge of the family and each member's ultimate destiny.

2. Parents are custodians of their children for a brief time of childrearing.
3. God has a purpose for parents independent of their children, and for their children independent of them.

When Parents Fail

We can't leave this topic without discussing the impact of genuine parental failure. So much of my counseling involves families where one or both parents have made serious errors either in child-rearing or in living a separated life.

A few years ago I counseled a family experiencing a truly unique situation.

The father had been in federal prison for the preceding eight years. Mom had stuck by him, raising their two daughters as a single parent while staying in touch with her husband through regular visits to the prison. The girls had even gone along a few time to see their dad.

Two months after Dad's much anticipated release, major problems broke out in the home.

This is where I entered the picture.

The older daughter, who was about fourteen at the time, could not accept her father's authority in the home. He had accepted Christ through a prison ministry and was trying to do the right thing now for his family, but his time away from them was a real obstacle. A solution was needed quickly because the daughter was threatening to run away the next time he tried to tell her what to do.

After several sessions dedicated to analyzing such variables as the family pattern of authority, their means and style of communication, and their problem-solving approach, I decided to focus on the fourteen-year-old more than her parents. As I saw it then, she did not understand her responsibility as a child in the home, a responsibility that included being obedient to her father as well as her mother.

After several sessions, we reached a point in counseling

40

where she began to accept and understand the responsibility she had for forgiving her father for his mistakes. Included was the need for her to avoid adding to the family adjustment difficulties by making unnecessary mistakes of her own. This young teenager needed to know that parents are people, too. She needed to understand that her responsibility in the family was not dependent on what her father had done years earlier. She was as bound by biblical principles as were her parents.

When parents fail, the family can be strengthened and grow from the experience if *God* is put back in control of the family. Certainly scars will remain, but they can be expected to fade with time just like physical scars.

Every member of the family unit must be willing to forgive any member of the family who fails. That means children must be able to forgive their parents and that parents should forgive children, and that children should forgive siblings.

Once we understand what God really expects of us as parents, once we remove our self-imposed conditions for family happiness, once we see what God desires for the family, then we can ask God for forgiveness for trying to do the job all alone. The curative elements of parental guilt include love, care, concern, and unselfishness. Added to this list is Christian commitment, spiritual growth, and the simple desire to be the best parents we can be. We all need to understand the impact of the positive qualities and the harm caused when they are left out of the family.

Points for Parents to Ponder

1. Do you often feel too weak to raise your children properly?

2. Before reading this chapter, did you think of your teenagers as just older children?

3. Were you and your spouse raised in a family where negotiation with parents was impossible?

4. When you reflect on yourself as a parent, does it make you more sad than happy?

5. Do you believe that you should be able to control the behavior of your children or teens all the time?

6. Do you believe there is a direct connection between perfect parenting and perfect children?

7. Do you see your worth or self-value measured by how your children turn out?

8. Is it impossible to be happy or content in the Lord while a child or teen is misbehaving?

9. Do you often feel that your children are more burden than blessing?

10. Do you believe that you are more responsible for your child or teen's behavior than they are?

("Yes" answers indicate tendency to accept the kind of parental guilt discussed in this chapter.)

3 / Family Dynamics

Sandra Thompson walks across the room to the bookcase where she picks up a family picture. In it she holds her infant daughter Cathy while the new father looks proudly down at them both.

Sighing, she sets the picture down. The peaceful atmosphere of that long-ago home has been transformed into a battlefield today. Sandra knew she had won this round with her rebellious teenage daughter, but she had been down this path too often to think that the war was won.

Sandra had over-reacted. *As usual*, she thought. Sixteen-year-old Cathy had just come in the house, full of weekend plans which had not been discussed with her mother. Sandra was sure that Cathy had not made more than a passing mention of the weekend to her mom, but she was always careful to insert that she had discussed it with her father and that everything was okay with him.

It was the same old treadmill, Sandra thought. She was so tired of the constant fighting.

And worse than anything, Sandra could not understand why she always seemed to feel so guilty when she and Cathy argued. "She's the one who's wrong," Sandra said aloud to herself. "So why do I always end up feeling guilty?"

Just then Cathy vaults from her bedroom and demands, "Where are my sweats?"

"What?" her mother answers.

"My sweats! I gave them to you this morning to wash!"

"I wash clothes on Saturdays, Cathy. You know that."

"But I need them tonight. I told you that!"

"You most certainly did not!" her mother retorts, getting ready to load the machine gun and put on her helmet as the battle approaches.

"Well, why would I give them to you this morning, special, if I didn't want them tonight? Honestly, anyone could figure that out!"

"That's enough of your insolence, young lady. Your sweats are in the laundry room. If you need them, you can wash them before supper."

"Well, I guess I'll have to," the girl responds.

"I don't know what the rush is anyway," Sandra responds, bringing up the reinforcements. "You're not going anywhere until your father and I talk about these plans of yours."

"I thought you're supposed to be a submissive wife, Mother."

Germ warfare, Mom thought, *totally outside the Geneva Conventions for conventional warfare.*

"If Daddy says I can go, you have to agree. Anyway, I'm leaving before he gets home."

"No, you're not. Call your friends and tell them to hold off."

"I can't do that and you know it. What are you going to do? Tie me up and lock me in my room until Daddy gets here? Well, you'll have to gag me, too, because I'll scream my head off when Tony and the others get here."

That's it! Nuclear weapons. End of battle!

Sandra turns and walks away, aware that she has lost. She certainly can't physically force her daughter to stay home. And Walt always managed to be late getting home whenever he suspected a battle awaited him. A phone call wouldn't help. He'd just say he was too busy to discuss it right now. They'd been over and over this. But he'd still be angry when he got home and found out what had taken place in his absence. And guess who would get the blame? That's right, Sandra.

"Now I know why some mothers abandon their families," she mumbles. "If it weren't for the boys, I might just leave myself." Even as she says it, Sandra knows she is seeing the same ominous signs in the boys. Sandra knows she shouldn't be surprised, but she is. And she's hurt and angry, too. Without having her heart in it, she begins to prepare the meal that nobody will feel like eating.

Children begin life totally submissive to parental will. But sooner or later, something happens to reduce that influence or eliminate parent power completely. In fact, the struggle can become so extreme that the children gain almost total control of the home and family. The roles are reversed from that of submissive child to submissive parent.

Walt and Sandra Thompson missed the parental control boat on two counts with Cathy. First of all, they were unprepared for the changes adolescence and puberty would bring in their daughter. In the second place, they hadn't learned how to exert their parental control so that the eventual departure from the family signaled by adolescence could be smooth.

The confrontation at the Thompson household may sound like a plot for the *Twilight Zone*, but it is reality in too many families. You probably know of similar situations. The ages and sex of the children may vary and the details may be a little different, but the theme is the same. Parents struggle to

45

maintain control of their homes and children, and the children and teens fight for greater independence. And it happens in the "best" of families.

The truth is that loss of parental control, influence, and power is probably the most common situation that brings families with youngsters in for counseling. I see it almost daily in the families with whom I work.

I also deal with powerless parents who suffer from the loss of self-esteem and self-respect because of their failure to parent properly. Such folks tend to be anxious, embarrassed, ashamed of their impotence, and desperate for a solution.

More than their relationship with their children is affected by their lack of influence and respect with their children. Their felt impotence corrodes their at-work performance, their Christian testimony, and even their marital relationship. I have known Christian fathers who began drinking because they couldn't face the loss of masculinity triggered when they could not get their children to behave.

Arguments between husbands and wives grow steadily worse as a child or teen's defiance increases. The air at the Thompson home was heavy with marital discord. Sandra Thompson cries out against her husband, "What's wrong with him? Why can't he be a man and get that child under control?"

If Walt Thompson agrees with his wife's perception of his parenting skills, his feeling of powerlessness increases. He is already caught in the bind of Cathy's manipulation. He is forced to react, and he may attempt to re-establish his power through assaults on his wife. He may try an extra-marital affair to prove to himself that he is still a man. He may try to beat the kids into submission. But more than likely, the other kids will simply learn to manipulate their father just as Cathy has done so efficiently.

Underpowered parents need help to rebuild their shattered self-concepts. Without renewed confidence in themselves and their ability to be in charge at home, even good counseling

46

won't help very much.

How can this overwhelming step be accomplished? What can help helpless parents? One approach is for parents to learn what the common causes of parent power failure really are, causes which are influenced by many things including the age of the child or teen involved.

Causes of Parental Power Loss

A definition may be helpful here. What is meant by parental power failure?

Power failures, outages the power company calls them, are the result of a parent's own responses to the guilt we experience because of the way we parent. It is important to recognize that our responses to our behavior cause the loss of power, not our responses to our children's behavior. In other words, we react to what *we* do in parenting, but we *think* we are reacting to what our children are doing.

This being the case, there is hope that if we can find a way to control our own reactions to our feelings, the result will be better behaved children and teens and happier homes. We are at risk for experiencing a vicious circle, though. Even as we lose power, we feel more and more guilty because down deep we know—or are afraid—that the problem lies in us and not in the children. We then search for someone to help us be better parents, and then we feel guilty because we need help to be better parents.

What needs to be changed are our feelings about what we are doing as parents. We have to understand that the guilty feelings we experience move us to search for "outside" answers. But most external plans fail because the family dynamics are not understood, and the cycle of guilt kicks in again. And we become increasingly powerless because of the guilt.

It sounds complicated, and perhaps it is, but we shouldn't

be surprised when it happens.

Let's get down to basics. As parents we need to back up and evaluate the basic proposition that parents are responsible for the behavior of their children.

First of all, we need to answer one major question: Does God intend that we have total or nearly total control over our children? Based on our answer to this question, we may need to make alterations in our attitude toward the job of parenting.

We also need to make a distinction between children and adolescents. Not the age difference necessarily, but the different ways we tend to lose influence with these two groups.

First, we must acknowledge that adolescents are truly young adults rather than old children. There is a difference. Teenagers have the mental ability to understand differently and thus respond differently than children.

With children, we lose power through the way we interact. With children, the crucial issue is: What is going on in the home (or not going on in the home) that is leading this child in such a negative direction?

Children subconsciously know ineffective parenting when they see it. It can take the form of poor methods, poor discipline, marital discord, inconsistency, and a multitude of others. The most obvious examples of poor parenting result from separation and divorce and from child abuse or incest.

With teenagers, parents lose power through the influence of friends, school, dates, drugs, alcohol, sexual temptation, and more. We also lose power to every individual teen's natural battle for greater independence.

That there should be a struggle is human nature. That parents should lose the struggle *is not* human nature or a godly nature. We are supposed to accept the battle for control of the family, but we are supposed to *win* that battle!

Let's examine the loss of parental power with children first.

Power Loss With Children

Children see themselves only as reflected in the eyes of their parents, and what they see controls and influences them as long as they live. Even under the most difficult, stressed, poverty-ridden and pessimistic conditions, parents are gods to their children. We are all-powerful, all-knowing, all-seeing. Who can keep a secret from one's mother? Who can get away with a lie when Mom or Dad looks you in the eye and asks for the truth? Who can defeat these giants?

Not me, says the young child. No way!

Parents are everything good and loving to young children. Parents possess all the warm fuzzies any child could ever want, and all a child has to do to get them is obey. How simple.

But then humanity begins to emerge from this toddler. The brain starts to work and the young child realizes that Mom and Dad are not gods, just big people. *People just like me, only much, much bigger and stronger.*

The preschooler actually tries to manipulate Mom and Dad, playing them one against the other. Tears flowing freely, the four-year-old says, "Daddy always gives me a cookie before I go to bed," and Mom wilts under her first experience with parental guilt and gives the cookie.

Parents lose power with older children for two basic reasons. The first deals with the role models we provide for our children. The second involves inefficient and/or inconsistent discipline. In other words, we parents lose power and influence with our children through our own acts of omission and commission rather than through outside influences, as is usually the case with teenagers.

Parents of young children teach them *everything* they believe about the world. We *are* their world for several years until they begin the process of bond-breaking with their first trip to school. We lose our influence only because we do not understand the nature of parental power and because we do not understand the nature of children. Once these concepts are grasped, as we will see throughout this book, power can be restored and additional power outages prevented.

Parental Modeling

Babies are often born with their eyes wide open, and to their parents, it seems that they never stop watching! Because we are our children's first heroes, children naturally seek to imitate what they see in us. They watch us, listen to us, and try to imitate us at every opportunity. Remember the son who was so proud when he picked up dad's hat and put it on to show the family? Or remember sis when she came out of the bedroom with mom's makeup all over her face?

Our kids naturally want to be just like us!

One thing that can greatly comfort suffering parents is the reassurance that even in the face of stress from a misbehaving son or daughter, the power of early parental modeling is stronger than any of us can imagine. Normally, we only see the true force of this as we watch our *grown* children becoming more and more like the parents they spent so many years arguing with as teenagers.

Unfortunately, we all have lapses in our parenting behavior that we wish our kids would *not* imitate. We have, over the years, modeled both good and bad behavior for our children. But for the parent experiencing the guilty-parent syndrome, the mind selects only those bad parental actions for memory replay.

But there is comfort, too.

Where parents tend to note and feel guilty about every failure, big or small, God looks on the "ways" of a person's life and tells us that these "macro" issues are of much more importance than the day-by-day "micro" issues.

What I am saying is that while God and good parents both care about the major and minor concerns of the family, we know both from the Bible and from observation that it is the entire course of one's life as a parent that has the greatest impact. As Solomon proclaimed in I Kings 8:39, "Then hear thou in heaven thy dwelling place, and forgive, and do, and give to every man according to his ways, whose heart thou knowest."

This passage and many others of a similar nature teach us that God is able to heal and forgive the effects of bad parenting. It is the "ways" of parenting that has the impact, much more so than the daily errors common to all families.

On the other hand, parental behavior can become so extreme that it can overwhelm a child's ability to bounce back. Compulsive overeating is one example of a problem common to Christian families who avoid some of the more "sinful" of the world's offerings. Overeating is an "acceptable" sin because eating habits and patterns are established early in life and prove to be exceptionally difficult to alter.

My family had such a problem when I was growing up. My parents were children during the depression of the thirties. It was natural for them to give my sisters and myself what they didn't have when they were children. My father had a particularly hard time as a child, and there were many days when hunger was the overriding concern in his home.

Consequently, food was in great abundance at our house. Consequently, too, we all have a weight problem. Although my parents were very good people who only wanted the best for their children, they provided a poor model for us on this issue. In essence, their example told us, "Eating is a great thing to do; don't worry about getting fat." So my sisters and I suffer varying degrees of overweight as adults.

Perhaps this might seem trivial. But it is a pattern which can have far-reaching results. We know that one of the prime factors in predicting future alcoholism is family background. This is especially true for boys growing up with alcoholic fathers. In spite of living with all the negative results of alcohol abuse including lost wages, personal disgrace, and child and spousal abuse, the children of alcoholic parents are far more likely to become alcoholics themselves compared to the children of non-drinkers.

The reason? Role modeling!

Other examples abound. Divorce, addictions, codependencies, violence, the list goes on and on. All are passed on in some degree to the children in the family. Parents who are poor examples for their children on a consistent basis (their ways, again) can be expected to experience a good bit of guilt at some point. The guilt may or may not be justified, of course, depending on the real or imagined nature of the parent behavior. But one thing is certain: If the damage did occur, it is extremely difficult to undo. Repentance and God's forgiveness are always available, of course, but the children may continue to suffer and the forgiven parent will continue to feel guilty to some degree.

If we parents are conscious of the fact that we are the ultimate role models for our children, we can be careful without becoming paranoid and self-doubting.

This process reminds me of an old television commercial, "Pay me now or pay me later." The message of that commercial could easily be applied to the example we set for our children and the guilt we feel when we have failed to live up to expectations...theirs or ours.

Whether we want to be or not, we are role models for our kids from the moment they are born until one of us dies. And even then, the last thing most Christian parents teach their children is how to leave this life and meet their Creator God.

Discipline and Control Methods

As I mentioned earlier, young children are controlled by the will of their parents more than the skill of their parents.

Any parent who wants to can control the behavior of a small child. And discipline and control are critical to the positive development of every child for many reasons, chief among them being the messages such behaviors send the children about the nature of their parents.

Children who experience firm and consistent discipline can normally be expected to acquire an adequate sense of security and love as a result. Firm, loving, flexible, and reasonable discipline tells any child that their parents care enough about them to spend time and effort helping them grow up well.

Although young children cannot articulate it yet, they understand that we love them when we care enough to take time with them. For children of any age, love is spelled T.I.M.E. Children who are loved will not be threatened by discipline. Children who are loved feel more loved after discipline, not less.

On the other hand, children who experience insufficient discipline receive the opposite message from their parents. Parents who "love their children too much to tell them 'no'" deliver the message: "I'm not sure of myself as a parent." They are saying, "I don't want to take a chance on making you dislike me."

We may also give children more credit than they deserve when we read our own feelings into our children and assume we all have the same mindset. In reality, children have only a child's frame of reference. One that is constantly developing and changing, but still distinctively child-oriented. We can save ourselves a considerable amount of unnecessary worry by realizing that our youngsters look at the world through immature, inexperienced eyes.

Parents who are able to function in a compassionate "control mode" with children will likely be rewarded with well-behaved, unsmothered children who give us little reason to feel guilty for being their parents.

53

Rules for Disciplining Children

The following suggested "rules" for administering discipline are known to be effective with normally functioning children. And please note that we are discussing disciplining *children*. We are *not* talking about teenagers. Not yet!

Be Flexible

Legalism in childrearing leads parents to perfectionistic attitudes. Childrearing legalism tells parents that if we do the right kind of job raising our children, they will not misbehave in any major way. They will be "perfect" in the area of major problems. Parents with this frame of mind set themselves up for serious guilt later when every child, teenager, or adult disappoints his or her parents.

When we tend toward legalism in discipline, we often tell ourselves that to be fair (legalistic) we must discipline each child the same and each offense must be handled the same way. To do otherwise would be "unfair." But not even the American system of justice does that. It allows people to plead mitigating circumstances, and God does not prescribe the same discipline for your sins as He might for mine. He understands our intentions, feelings, and motives, then disciplines His children in His own creative, individual ways.

When we find cases of child abuse in Christian families, and it is not as uncommon as we might want to believe, it is usually a result of the parent's attitude that being flexible is somehow sinful. In my experiences as a counselor I have dealt with dozens of child abuse cases in Christian families. Each one occurred because of excessive, inflexible, unreasonable, and harsh discipline methods.

Flexibility covers both the type of discipline and the method of delivering that discipline. What is needed for a given child? Corporal punishment? Withdrawal of privileges? A stern "talking to"?

And how should the discipline be administered? Should

Mom or Dad do it? If it is a spanking, should it be with a hand, a paddle, or a switch? Should the grounding be for one day or for life?

Children do not benefit from discipline. They benefit from *good* discipline—discipline that takes their ages and circumstances into consideration. Children benefit from being disciplined the way that God disciplines us, His children— carefully, patiently, compassionately, and physically only when everything else has failed...or that's the only way we'll listen.

Be Quick

The principle is simply this: The shorter the time span between an act and its consequences, the greater the learning.

We are raising children who may not yet have the ability to understand all the why's and wherefore's of what Mom and Dad are doing. This is especially true when it comes to discipline. With young children in particular, memory and understanding are both limited. The longer a young child has to think about what he did wrong, the more he will forget and the more he will be confused when the discipline finally arrives.

Parents, however, must be careful to discipline only when their anger has subsided, when they are fully in control of their own emotions and actions and know exactly what they are doing. Discipline administered when Mom or Dad is angry can produce life-long damage in a child if it is uncontrolled. It also invariably leads to parental guilt which will make future discipline even more difficult to do right.

Deliberately making the child wait for discipline not only reduces the amount and quality of learning, but it also leans in the direction of "cruel and unusual punishment." We need to make an executive parental decision about the need for and type of discipline, act on that decision, and forget it. This is how God deals with us when we need chastening. A wise parent will want to do the same with his or her children. Remember, too, that *children* here means pre-adolescents as well.

Be Consistent

Children can adjust to almost anything except inconsistent and unpredictable parents. They can adjust to very harsh parents and to very lenient parents, but children cannot adjust to parents who are harsh one day and lenient the next. My parents were on the lenient side with me, the oldest child and only boy, while my wife's parents were relatively strict with her, the younger of two sisters. We each found different ways of coping with our parents, and we could do so because our parents were predictable and consistent.

When parents are unpredictable, children are put in what psychologists call a "double-bind" situation. Children need to make decisions in order to mature well, but expecting them to sense the mood of a parent and react accordingly is simply unrealistic. Children placed in this kind of confusing situation run the risk of becoming depressed, shy, withdrawn, and in extreme cases, even suicidal.

We can be flexible without becoming unpredictable, merciful without being inconsistent. If something was wrong yesterday, a child will expect it to be wrong today, too. If the punishment for backtalk was grounding last week, it should be grounding this week. But at the same time, we need to be fair and merciful, reflecting God's mercy and grace to us as parents and as *His* children. God considers circumstances and intentions as He deals with us. We should do the same as we deal with others.

Power Outages With Teenagers

Many avenues exist for power loss with teenagers. The focus of life for teens today is outside the home and family. Parents should expect to experience gradually less and less influence as the children grow and become adolescents and young adults. But if we have done a credible job of parenting, we won't *need* as much power or influence. Our young adults will make their own, responsible decisions.

But a power loss that results in a teenager determining the direction of life for the family is not acceptable. When parents of teens surrender their God-given and God-*required* responsibility for decision-making to a teenager, we create immense potential for problems that may go far beyond the boundaries of the individual household.

We can be balanced parents, still in control of the home and family as God expects, yet be flexible and tolerant of the teenagers in the home who are trying to establish themselves as young adults preparing for life on their own.

Friends

Probably nothing is more useful for teenagers trying to make their parents feel guilty than friends.

"But, Mom, *all* the kids are wearing these to school."

"But, Dad, *all* the other parents let their kids my age stay out until 1:00 a.m. on weekends."

Of course the implied message in these whiny pleadings is that if you don't let me do what *all* the other kids are doing, *you*, Mom and Dad, will feel guilty.

And you know what?

It usually works!

The life focus of teenagers moves from family to friends quickly and completely, but usually not permanently. While younger children normally gravitate to their parents' arms out of love and a need to feel safe and protected, adolescents are discovering a perception shift that shows their parents as incredibly old and out of touch with reality, and they seem to have become incredibly stupid almost overnight. We suddenly look old-fashioned, unrealistic, unsympathetic and senile to the point of not understanding anything about young people. Besides that, teens realize how funny Mom and Dad have been dressing all these years.

But that's okay!

We felt the same way about our parents, too. We've just forgotten.

But while all this new parental perception stuff is going on, friends have also been transformed. The other kids have been converted from convenience beings, there when they wanted someone to play with, to the coolest beings—worldly wise, great looking, happy, unselfish, and generally the best thing since sliced bread!

And don't forget, teenagers have no acquaintances. Every warm body of the same general age known to the teen is counted as a friend. If we ask our teens to tell us how many friends they have, they will count every teenager they know who is not an enemy or a total loser.

The significance of all this is that these friends become the standard by which parents are evaluated. You and I are graded according to what the other parents are doing. If we are not careful, this can become a major component in the guilty-parent syndrome.

Know what is *really* going on. Call the other parents to check. You will probably find out that what you are doing is very much in line with most of the other kids' parents, even though our kids hope against hope that we never find that out.

Parents can plan ahead to accept the importance of friends. It is not reasonable to expect to have the same influence with a teenager as you do with a child. But then, again, we should not *need* the same influence if we have parented adequately.

We can, for example, allow our teen to invite friends over for a get-together of some sort. We can let our teens' friends see us as we are: normal, average, optimistic, reasonable, not-a-bullwhip-in-sight parents. We want to be parents who do not *need* to be involved in every aspect of our child's life in order to feel comfortable with the family or to feel that we still have a measure of control.

But when we come face to face with a different reality, a different strategy is needed.

Suppose your teen is running with kids you *know* are unacceptable? What can you do?

You can ask open-ended questions, in hopes of encouraging your teenager to reflect on what he is doing and who he is doing it with. We do *not* want to challenge or confront outright because teenagers will universally rise to the defense of their friends even when they know that Mom and Dad are right. There is something in the heart of most teens that makes it very hard to agree with one's parents.

Controversial friends will be defended because adolescents are capable of intense loyalty, even when they know their friends are wrong. Teens also feel peer pressure and react protectively toward their friends. In fact, negative or controversial friends are often acquired by teens because they are interesting, different, and status-enhancing. Parents need to recognize this to avoid feeling guilty when their kids fail to measure up in these areas.

When confronted with a problem of this type, we must first resist the temptation to over-react. Our teens will, in the majority of families, have their parents' values and standards, *eventually*! We need to proceed cautiously when dealing with negative peer pressure and friends so that we do not turn the situation into a crisis. And we want to remember that down deep, we are still the most important people in the world to our kids. They are just having a hard time admitting that right now.

School

School and friends are closely related for most teens. For now, we'll consider the influence of schooling itself rather than the social aspects of the school environment.

I taught junior high school for five years in Detroit. I was also a counselor in the same school for two years and assistant principal there for one year. But my children were in Christian schools all that time. Through this experience I learned that *both* public and private schools can present problems for parents of teens that could easily lead to profound feelings of parental guilt.

All schools invariably teach values. No exceptions. Students in all school systems are taught the values of their teachers. Children enrolled in a public school will absorb ideas and concepts their parents might not like. But this can also be true in Christian or other private schools.

Parents shouldn't feel guilty because a public school is the only thing available in the area, or because they cannot afford the extra expense of a private school. We have found that all too many Christian parents rely too heavily on the school to do their parenting for them in the spiritual and moral areas of life.

The point is that a few hours a day, usually six or seven out of twenty-four, for no more than forty out of fifty-two weeks a year, should not be sufficient to overwhelm all the years of teaching the children received before they began school nor should those hours overwhelm the other eighteen hours a day when the kids are home with Mom and Dad.

We often feel guilty about this issue, and just as often, the guilt is not warranted! Our power and influence with our children will *not* be smothered by what happens at school. If the situation there gets truly bad, speak to the school board and watch how fast things change in your favor.

Media

We are really only discussing television and movies right now, although there are other forms of media like radio that may be important.

But for today's kids, television and movies are the prime

source of entertainment. We can speak of these two forms in the same breath because of the great popularity of VCRs in the last few years.

Parents must make a conscious choice to have a role in choosing forms of entertainment for their kids. Failure to exercise this influence is an admission to the child or teen that we either do not care what they watch or believe that it makes no difference.

If this is the case in your home, you *ought* to be feeling guilty about it and move to change it!

Who rents the VCR movies that are viewed in your home? Who pays for them? Who decides what TV programs will or will not be watched? If the answer to all these questions is not parents, that family is in trouble and headed for more.

Mom and Dad must have the courage to say a firm "no" when we feel convicted about a movie or TV program. Our kids will rise up and thank us *later*, and we won't add fuel to the guilty-parent syndrome.

Work

A common source of parental guilt relates to requests by teenagers for an after-school job. We feel guilty if we say yes, and then we feel guilty if we say no! This can be a tough call for many families.

The problem is, we know that it is generally good for teenagers to work outside the home. But the job cannot be allowed to take over the adolescent's life. Jobs can become monsters if we aren't careful and can influence every aspect of a teen's life. Dating, church, family activities, chores, and many more valuable experiences can become victims of the teen's need to work.

Work for teens should only be allowed as long as grades do not drop. If their behavior at home and school remains acceptable and the push for independence does not threaten to overwhelm long-range plans for college and the like, work

61

is beneficial. They will be more grown-up, develop better social skills, develop a better self-concept, and be better prepared to face the responsibilities of life after adolescence.

Linda and I encouraged our three children to work during their last two years of high school.

For Laurie, our oldest, work was positive. Her grades stayed where they should be; she didn't ask to be let out of family activities or responsibilities, and she spent and saved her money wisely.

But then there was Doug!

Good old Doug wanted a car worse than anything in this world. He eventually lined up a job making pizzas during the eleventh grade, saved his money, and got a car. But we battled Doug over grades, curfew, and lots of things that probably could have been postponed or avoided if he had not worked. For Doug, work was both positive and negative: positive because he was more mature and acted it; negative because he dropped out of sports and focused on the car too much.

And Jennifer, our last, could not work in high school because of her musical involvement.

Parents feel guilty about this issue when the decisions produce results other than what we anticipate. But parenting is a trial-and-error process, so let's not feel guilty when we don't have to!

Church

Whether or not you are surprised to find church listed as a potential source of parental guilt depends on how long you have been a Christian, how old your children are, and what kind of church your family attends.

Church activities can become a pseudo-family in some circumstances. Excessive time spent either away from the family or with the family away from home may indicate that a problem is developing. Have you ever noticed that whenever you read about a cult, it always involves either the families moving in together into a commune kind of environment or the breaking up of families because a pastor/leader is telling folks that their church is more important than their family?

Church is a special place for special times and must never replace the home and family as the primary reference point for living. While there is a social aspect, church is a place of corporate worship, to honor God.

Of course, a good Bible-believing church and pastor ought to minister to us by illuminating the truths of God's Word. We can all learn more about being godly parents as we become more Christ-like people, and a good church should be an arm of the family in raising children in the nurture and admonition of the Lord. But even the influence of the church can be harmful if allowed to get out of balance, creating a loss of parental power and the resulting strong guilt feelings.

Plans and step-by-step procedures are often offered as solutions to *any* family's problems. We are told, "Follow these steps and your problems will vanish." But if these plans and procedures were as effective as they are proclaimed to be, why are they not spelled out in the Bible? We must also ask: How have these "experts" done with their own families? Is the expert even married or a parent?

Good pastors and family counselors know that family problems cannot be resolved outside the family and without knowing *a great deal* about the individual family and the individual members. Of course, help may be needed at various points, especially with teenagers, but the primary change-agents for any family must be the parents. Christian families support the local church and the local church supports the family. When we get those out of balance, feelings of parental guilt always follow.

Family Break-up

I am not sure if it is wise to save the worst for last, but this is what I've done. A family break-up has the most far-reaching effects on *all* the family members, but what is often overlooked is the impact of divorce on the parents. Guilt is clearly the single greatest emotion experienced by divorced and divorcing parents, and often the guilt is justifiable.

I recognize that while it takes two to make a marriage, it often takes only one to make a divorce. Every parent needs to take a long look at the future damage potential of this decision *before* it's made.

Our churches have acknowledged the prevalence of divorce as well. When was the last time you heard your pastor preach against divorce? Maybe your church is different than most, but in too many, divorce is an accepted, though unwanted, reality of life.

Divorce is a threat to the survival of not only the family but also of the local church. Divorce is the ultimate breakdown of the family unit, leaving more and more children in single parent homes. And single parenting *often* is a negative factor in the lives of children and teens. Ninety-two percent of the time, Mom is the custodial parent, and after two years, *most* dads have no further contact with their children.

Children suffer; Mom suffers; Dad suffers; society suffers, and the church suffers. There is a lot of guilt to go around with divorce, and nothing promotes the guilty-parent syndrome like losing one's family to divorce.

A Final Word

In my own family and in the hundreds of families with whom I've worked through the years, parent guilt stems more from a sense of powerlessness than it does from actual failures in parenting.

This sense of powerlessness can be seen in many ways: frustration over a rebellious teenager, anger caused by an apparently uncontrollable child, or embarrassment when others become aware of *my* child's misbehavior.

Guilt is painful for parents. When we are in pain, we seek

relief. Seeking relief can lead to "quick fix solutions" that only make the matter worse in the long run.

Legitimate solutions to problems of power failure and parental guilt do exist. But for most of us, when all is said and done, we will realize that what we are going through as parents is what God *expects* of us in raising *His* children.

Points for Parents to Ponder

1. Like Sandra Thompson, do you wish for the "good old days" when the children were younger?

2. Do you feel guilty when you tell your youngster "no," even though you are sure that it is best?

3. Have you experienced similar feelings to those of Sandra Thompson in her confrontation with her daughter?

4. If the answer to number three is yes, did you also give in?

5. Do you often feel that the kids are putting a strain on your marriage?

6. Were you and/or your spouse raised by very powerful or very weak parents?

7. Do your children play one parent against another?

8. Does the idea that you are a model or an example for your children make you uncomfortable?

9. Is it hard for you to accept the principle that God will forgive your mistakes in parenting?

10. Did you feel cheated out of spending time with your parents when you were a child?

("Yes" answers indicate tendencey to accept the kind of parental guilt discussed in this chapter.)

4 / Guilt-Free Parenting Principles

Sally Johnson is a single parent, trying to raise three children on her own since the divorce. She recently moved in with her mother, also divorced, and her mother's fifteen-year-old son Brad. Sally's children include thirteen-year-old Larry, his ten-year-old brother Eddy, and Jennifer, about six.

Sally is on welfare, Aid To Dependent Children, and works full time in a convenience store close to the mobile home she shares with her mother. The living conditions for these two families in one trailer are horrendous!

One bathroom for six people, a smaller than average trailer, and Sally and her three children actually sleeping in the same room, virtually on the same bed. They're on the waiting list for independent public housing, but in the rural area where they live, the wait is very long.

Sally brought Larry in to see me because of school misbehavior, extremely poor grades, and growing disobedience at home. After listening to Sally's story and seeing Larry a few times, I asked Sally to return for a session without her son.

I needed to tell this single mother that Larry was reacting more or less normally to a very stressful situation. Just into puberty with all the normal young adolescent needs for privacy and a sense of independence, Larry was "burned-out" with his living conditions. I assured Sally that I would keep working with Larry for as long as was needed, but I didn't think the situation would improve as long as their living arrangements remained as they were.

Larry was subconsciously striking back at the environment facing him, and until that environment changed in some major way, the problems would not change very much either.

Like Sally, many parents, single or married, experience a variety of "power outages" that could be prevented. Once lost, influence with children or teenagers can be extremely difficult to regain. Parents who are tough and then loosen up, discover that they cannot go back to stricter rules without causing major upheavals. Once the rules have been softened, the parents are "stuck" with the consequences.

Power is lost through some of the following "outages":
1. Poor parenting techniques.
2. Inconsistent or unreasonable discipline.
3. Marital difficulties.
4. The intrusion of the media into family life and values.
5. An inheritance of a negative attitude toward and about children.
6. And a host of others that you could suggest.

Ineffective parenting produces strain on any marriage, stress for the children who feel a loss of security, school-related problems, and a lowered quality of life for the entire family.

Consider the attitude of God toward Abraham and his family in Genesis 18:19 and ask yourself if God could say such things about *your* family.

"For I know him, that he will command his children and his household after him, and they shall keep the way of the Lord, to do righteousness and judgment; that the Lord may bring upon Abraham that which he hath spoken of him."

Consider how far from this example was Sally and her family. Certainly it was not all of her own making, yet the Bible gives us firm ideas about retaining our ability to influence our children, to "command" them as mentioned in the passage above.

Sally is going to remain ineffective as a mother as long as she feels guilty. And she will feel guilty as long as her living conditions remain the same. A bitter and unhappy cycle, I know, but perhaps we can learn something from this sad situation that will encourage us to implement the following ideas.

Guilt-Free Power-Based Parenting Principles

Principle #1: Parents should work *with* rather than *against* their children and teens.

Most parents find the "Pygmalion Effect" of turning a loser into a winner to be very true with their kids and kids in general just because they believe the kids can do it. For the most part, a young person will live up–or down–to his parents' expectations of him.

The behavior we expect is usually the behavior we receive.

Believing that children will give us trouble and teenagers will give us *lots* of trouble virtually guarantees the truth of that idea. This is so because such a belief sets an "adversarial mind-set" in children and their parents and becomes almost an undeclared war.

Over the years I have been counseling, I have been surprised at how often I see this reflected in comments from parents.

"Well, we should have expected trouble when he became a teenager."

"We were warned to watch out for the 'adolescent crazies' and here they are!"

"I just knew my son was going to rebel at some point. I guess I shouldn't be surprised."

Expecting a struggle brings a struggle. But expecting calm, reasoned behavior from children and adolescents will also *usually* bring about better behavior. Of course, some kids are going to rebel and have some problems no matter what their parents do. But the damage and turmoil is *minimized* when we have high but reasonable expectations for the youngsters in the family. Be careful to avoid an adversarial relationship in the family!

Principle #2: Giving, not receiving, is the goal of good parenting.

Our pastor in Detroit was fond of saying that the only way to loan money to a family member or friend is to assume that you are really just giving the money away as a gift. Any other approach results in worry and resentment over something that didn't have to be done in the first place.

The same holds true with our kids. When families get the giving/receiving order reversed in a family, trouble *always* follows. We are to expect *nothing* from our children. We can desire that our children love us, obey us, honor us, be loyal to us, and so on, but if we get to the point where we think that we *deserve* these things independent of our own behavior, we are in trouble ourselves. Parents must work to maintain the love, respect, honor, obedience, and loyalty of their children.

To believe that our children must love us simply because we are their parents is unwise and counterproductive. Should a father who is sexually abusing a daughter demand that she love him? Should a mother who is beating her eight-year-old son expect that he should still love her in spite of the beatings? Should a parent who has abandoned the family return after

70

a long absence and expect to be welcomed with open arms? Of course not. You and I could never do this.

The Bible does spell out actions required of good children, but problems arise when a parent believes that the children and teens were given to him or her by God to meet *their needs*, rather than they to meet the needs of their children.

It is through our unconditional gift of love for our children, modeling God's great love for us (Romans 5:8), that we can expect them to reciprocate with obedience. But love that is not unconditional is nothing more than a bribe to children, telling them that, "You are here for my purposes and to meet my needs. I love you, yes, but only when you do as I say." Giving is always and only parent to child.

Principle #3: Husband/wife cooperation is necessary for guilt-free Christian parenting.

Simple agreement, important as it is when it comes to children, is not proof of cooperation. What Mom and Dad need to do is *really* agree about the kids rather than one threaten the other or psychologically or spiritually force the other into agreement. Parents lose parental effectiveness, in part, through allowing the kids to know that they disagree about how to deal with them in some important area. Children and teens will use a "divide and conquer" strategy to insert a wedge between Mom and Dad.

God established a two-parent system for raising children. I don't know why God ordained that there be only men and women and one of each for parents. It is interesting, if a little foolish, I'll admit, to speculate on what the world would have been like if God had decided to have five sexes instead of two. I've thought about it, but not for very long!

In any case, *true* parental cooperation is essential in child-rearing. Presenting a united front is especially important for teens and pre-teens who are probably thinking about ways to assert their budding feelings of independence. Children and teens will exploit perceived weaknesses in parents, even when unaware that they are doing so.

Lack of true cooperation produces ineffective parenting. Ineffective parenting leads to feelings of guilt, making good parenting even less likely. But when parents are united in spirit as well as behavior, even the most rebellious teenager or disobedient child knows the battle is lost.

Principle #4: Mistakes in parenting are both expected and correctable.

The perfect parent is yet to be created! We know for sure that it won't be you or me! And there is some comfort in the knowledge that the only mistakes that become major guilt-producers are those that remain uncorrected for long periods of time.

In the final analysis, God has prepared each of us to be able to meet the needs of our children. Because of this assurance, we can rest in the knowledge that God also knows our weak points and failings but trusts us to be good parents anyway.

Perfection is an unbiblical goal of parenting. Expectations of perfection, or even near-perfection, always result in feelings of failure and guilt. We can be good parents without being perfect parents, and when being good is good enough, we will be better than we thought possible.

Principle #5: Parents are not responsible for the happiness of their children at any age.

Happiness is not a goal but a by-product of Christian living. This, plus the reality that one human being cannot ever *make* another human happy, allows Christian parents to set reasonable goals for themselves.

This issue is important. A major contributor to parental guilt is the feeling that results when one of our children is unhappy. Feeling responsible (thus guilty) when a child is unhappy because of a rule or requirement encourages us to soften or break those rules when they should remain strong. Feeling guilty for an unhappy child, assuming that Mom or Dad are *not* involved in abuse and other such behaviors, is simply unreasonable and unfair to parents.

Parents who experience this kind of guilt are vulnerable to trying to "buy" happiness for the kids with things and activities. Of course, children and teens are pleased to receive gifts; no young person will tell you he doesn't want to be spoiled because he knows it's not good for him. But children and teens will not *stay* happy because of things. Yet this is the trap many of us fall into. Once we try to buy a cheerful disposition, we are inviting exploitation by our youngsters.

Teachers and child-care providers know that the least happy kids are those who come from over-indulgent homes. Things become symbols that, "Mom and Dad love me," leading children to lose contact with the real signs of love. They are themselves prone in later years to try to buy respect, love, and attention through bribing others in the same way.

Principle #6: Parents must develop a sense of humor about parenting.

If we think about it for a minute, parenting is a ridiculous thing to ask anyone to do. Parents are expected to love and support these miniature people for eighteen years or longer, in spite of the fact that many of them won't appreciate even half of it and may actively rebel.

Kids are bound, some think genetically programmed, to do the strangest things in the process of becoming adults. If we can maintain a sense of humor, the problems will lose some of their power to depress us parents.

Let's face it, parents are prone to something called "parental amnesia," an affliction known to cause long lapses in memory at the time those memories would be most valuable. We tend to forget how we dealt with our own parents. What we did on *our* dates. What kinds of things we did that scared our parents to death but didn't mean much to us at the time. I am middle-age, and there are some things my parents *still* don't know about.

Principle # 7: Good parenting requires that parents set time aside for their children rather that trying to squeeze children into a crowded schedule.

Functional families *always* find a way to set aside time for the children. *Always!*

Special time with parents, even if it is only fifteen minutes of undistracted story-time at bedtime, tells children that they are an important priority in the family. It tells them that they take precedence over phone calls from strangers, the television news, a mini-series on TV, or a good book waiting to be read. Special time gives parents an opportunity to find out what is on the child's mind and goes a long way toward convincing teens and pre-teens that someone really does care about their problems and concerns.

This individual time should be both special and routine. The bedtime story should be routine. But there should also be special activities with the family, and once in a while with *just one of the children.* Parents sometimes err in assuming that treating one child to a special day will make the others feel bad. It will not, providing they each have *their* special day, too!

Principle #8: Guilt-free parents are disciplined disciplinarians.

Discipline here refers to self-discipline as well as child or teen discipline. I ushered with a father some years back who had a reputation in the church as a very strict, stern, unbending disciplinarian. He was a good man in most ways, but I felt he was reflecting the kind of parenting he had been exposed to as a child, and I thought this was the reason he failed to see the inconsistency in his behavior.

He was inconsistent because in spite of being very "disciplinarian" in his attitudes, he was about 80 pounds overweight and was notorious at church activities and other gatherings for being able to "out eat" everybody. His children are now grown up, and I have often wondered at what age they began to rebel over being disciplined by an un-self-disciplined father.

Parents who are disciplined disciplinarians teach by their discipline and by their example. Parents who are self-disciplined disciplinarians do a lot *less* disciplining, especially when the kids become teenagers!

Principle #9: Guilt-free parenting is educated parenting.

We all know people who are educated but have never been "schooled." We are just as likely to know people, probably many more, who have been schooled without ever being educated.

Educated parents are not only those with multiple college degrees. They are parents who are able to learn from the trial-and-error process called parenting. Educated parents are those who can make adjustments without feeling as if they have surrendered. An educated parent is one who can integrate appropriate Bible teachings with modern research on the family and not feel a need to apologize for doing so. An educated parent is one who can tell a child, "I'm sorry. I was wrong."

Points for Parents to Ponder

1. Do you feel less "powerful" now compared to when the children were younger?

2. Can you identify with any of the "power outages" listed in this chapter?

3. Would you say that you are more pessimistic than optimistic when it comes to your children? In other words, is your parenting "glass" half-full or half-empty?

4. Do you often feel lilke an "adversary" with your children?

5. Do you believe children are here to help meet the needs of their parents?

6. Do you feel that you get less support than you need from your spouse?

7. Are mistakes a sign of parental failure?

8. Are you surprised that some people can joke about their experiences as a parent?

9. Are you very overweight?

10. Would you characterize your parenting as very authoritiarian or very permissive?

("Yes" answers indicate tendency to accept the kind of parental guilt discussed in this chapter.)

5 / Parenting Styles

In order to understand this process of guilt reduction in a family setting, we need to consider our individual "style" of parenting and what it means. Self-awareness is a must.

Parent style refers to the dominant personal philosophy each parent employs in dealing with dependent children and teenagers. Parent style is the mindset, the basic foundational attitude that distinguishes one parent from another. Parent style is important because my parent style and yours result invariably from *our* experiences as children being raised by our own set of parents. Parent style is the customary, everyday way we have of dealing with our children and teens and that holds very long-term implications for our kids.

Developmental experts concur that there are anywhere from three to ten or more different "styles" of parenting. The styles have different names, and there is a lot of overlap between them sometimes, but they all agree on the importance of parental self-awareness on this issue. Our self-awareness is a crucial factor in our becoming a powerful and guilt-free force for good in the lives of our children. Parent style *is* predictive of the future behavior of our children. And parent style can be altered and adjusted only to the extent that the parent is aware of what he is doing and why.

Democratically Oriented Parents

Parents demonstrating a democratic orientation toward their children and teens tend to be supportive and affirmative, looking more at a youngster's potential for good than the possibility of evil. Such parents believe in discipline but practice a form of child control with broad limits and wide tolerance for trial-and-error growing. Democratically oriented parents believe young people of all ages are capable of thoughts and ideas worthy of adult attention.

Democratically oriented parents tend to produce young people characterized as outgoing, popular, reasonably self-confident, and independent. These characteristics tend to show up at an early age compared to other children. Children raised in this manner tend to expect to be treated with age-appropriate respect by others and might have difficulty in very strict circumstances such as military schools and legalistically oriented schools and colleges.

Authoritarian Parenting

Authoritarian parents are very different from democratically oriented parents. Authoritarian parents tend toward being rigid and controlling with their youngsters, leaning toward the belief that children and teens must be protected from themselves. Control is the operative term with authoritarian parents who measure their success as parents by the outward behavior of their children at any age.

Children from authoritarian homes tend to be more on the shy, withdrawn side, especially females, and may even be neurotic and self-critical. Authoritarian parents tend to have well-behaved children and poorly behaved adolescents where democratically oriented parents tend to have rambunctious children but better behaved adolescents.

Indulgent Parents

The third of the three broad types of parenting is the indulgent parent. While often called "spoilers" by others, indulgent parents may or may not be as "loose" as some assume. I personally know quite a few parents I would classify in this category, and most of them have very well-behaved children *and* teenagers. Of course, their day-by-day tolerance for messiness or loud playing may not suit you or me, but in the long run, the indulgent parent produces a better *grown* offspring than more authoritarian parents.

What most of us who criticize indulgent parents really mean is the *over-indulgent* parent who gives in to all child or teen demands more out of a basic fear of the young person than a desire to make them happy. This fear explains why so many *over*-indulged young people turn on the very parents who gave them everything they wanted. What these young people realize is that their parent or parents did not really love them but were simply trying to buy their love and obedience. That never works for very long.

But children raised by a more reasonable form of indulgent parent do pretty well and tend to grow up to be more independent than others of the same age and better able to deal with adults. These kids can become antisocial and rebellious if circumstances are suitable, but most seem to do all right.

Where Do You Place Yourself?

Can you find one of these categories that comes close to what you and your spouse practice in your family?

Most importantly, are you satisfied with the results you are obtaining with your children?

What we need to remember is that the critical factor in

being a guilt-free parent is self-awareness. Couple this with a willingness to make small adjustments to meet the differing needs of different children in your family, and we are on the right track. In families that are led by two parents, if there is an extreme tendency in one, the other will likely soften that tendency. I know that I tend to be the indulgent parent in my family. Thankfully, God provided me with Linda who tends to be the tough guy, and we balance one another pretty well. Like you and your spouse, we have differing but complementary ideas about children and child-rearing, and we understand why God ordained that children be raised by two parents.

For example, when our children were teenagers (one still is), certain rules applied. When they were out on a date or with their friends somewhere, they needed to call home if they wanted to change their plans or come in later than had been agreed. A predictable pattern developed. The phone would ring, Linda would answer it, and our son or daughter would ask for me. And they had their reasons. They knew that my approach with them was to ask, "Is there any reason you should not do what you are asking to do?" They would answer and explain, and I would generally agree with some qualifications.

They knew that if they had to do the explaining to their mother, they would have to offer long, complex, analytical discourses on the pros and cons of such a request. It was not unusual that if I was not available, they would just say to their mother, "Oh, that's all right. I'll be home on time."

My philosophy was to say yes unless there was a reason to say no. Linda's position was (and is) to say no unless there is a reason to say yes. Our kids did okay because each of our positions moderated the other's.

Parents should not expect to be able to place themselves exclusively in one category or another. It's just not that clear cut in most families. But we all need to recognize that a major portion of our parental influence comes from our individual parenting style. If your parenting seems weak at the moment, perhaps an adjustment is in order.

Powerful and Understanding Parenting

When parents are faced with a difficult situation involving child or adolescent behavior, we sometimes need to be reminded that we are, in fact, more powerful, more intelligent, more experienced, and more spiritually wise than they are. Parenting skill is very important, but it is totally ineffective without the will to do what needs to be done.

Part of the process of building will into Christian parenting is learning enough about the family to feel confident. Parental will is established through education and experience regarding motivation for wrongdoing. Once motivation is understood, we parents can begin to feel more as if we are in charge. When we feel as if we know what we are doing, our kids sense this and react with more acceptable behavior.

Will and skill are fine, but we also need to think about why children and teens misbehave in the first place.

For one thing, because they are human!

Humanity bestows on each of us the burdensome tendency to give in to the base nature in all of us. Children never need instruction on how to get into trouble, do they? Quite the contrary, they need constant instruction in how to stay *out* of trouble. Within the realm of reasonableness, we understand the need for certain levels of control on all people of all ages, simply because we all fall short at times of what God and society expect of us. But there are other reasons for misbehavior.

Many youngsters misbehave simply to get attention. Feeling left out or rejected is about the most powerful emotion possible for a child or teenager. The desire to avoid feeling this pain motivates many kids to give in to "peer pressure," and then they find themselves in trouble of some

81

kind. These kids would rather get the attention of their friends than feel left out. This is why peer pressure is so powerful.

And if we are talking about younger children, we know that they will usually trade a spanking for parental attention. Feeling ignored hurts worse than a spanking, and kids feel that negative attention, if that's all they can get, is better than no attention. This is one reason spankings and other forms of discipline sometimes fail to stop bad behavior. There may be nothing at all wrong with the method, but Mom or Dad simply plays into the child's hands by giving them the attention they have misbehaved to get. Paying attention only to bad behavior can become a major problem if it isn't stopped. "Catch them being good" is the answer to negative-attention behavior.

Children and teens also misbehave out of a need for feelings of power. Children and adolescents need to feel that they make a difference, and the family, school, church, or neighborhood provide the "proving grounds" for young people to test their power. Power motivation is universal, and parents should encourage the correct kind of controlled power rather than trying to stifle all expressions of power in youngsters.

Parents and other adults can encourage a positive use of power by taking opportunities that present themselves. For example, children can be asked how they feel about the family's choice of a vacation this year. They can go along when Mom and Dad look at new cars. Kids at almost all ages except the very young should be allowed to help pick out their school clothes.

I can almost hear some saying, "But I already do these things. And more!"

Good!

My guess is that those of us who already do these things have very little serious trouble getting children to obey when it comes to unpleasant things like cleaning out the garage or cutting the grass. Children can feel influential without being the controlling force, and that's good for everyone.

Young people have an expression. "What goes around, comes around," and this saying fits exactly what we are talking about here. A mom and dad who are able to give kids a sense of power and influence will receive implicit permission from the kids to exercise greater power and influence with them. It's all up to Mom and Dad and how they manage these issues in the family.

On the down side, there are many kids who act out and misbehave from a need to get even for some real or imagined wrong. This is particularly common where the family has undergone some trauma such as divorce, unemployment, a death, or even changing residences and schools. Excessive and harsh punishment also generates negative results for the family.

But parents who have established open patterns of communication during the early years can expect to have far fewer problems in the later years. Children and teenagers expressing the difficulties above tend to come from families where open and free communication is not the norm and where young people are not talked *with* on a regular basis. They tend to think, sometimes correctly, that no one cares what they think anyway.

Finally, children and teens misbehave because they believe that is what is expected of them. I hope this sounds foreign to your family because it means your family will experience much less difficulty. But many do have a problem with negative expectations and, sadly, this often brings with it lifelong problems.

When young people acquire a negative self-concept, the kind that grows from pessimistic parenting, we know that two things at least are true. We know that the negative self-concept was probably developed through the parenting style and attitudes of the parents and that the negative self-concept and defeatism is unlikely to change if it continues into adolescence.

This is tough parenting and strong realities, but if we want to parent our children in a guilt-free manner, it has to be faced and recognized so we can make sure it doesn't happen in our families or to stop it if we see any symptoms of it. We know that healing a breach in family relationships caused by pessimistic parenting is very difficult at best. The key is to block the development of negative self-concepts by correcting pessimistic parenting. Pessimistic parenting is guilt-based and guilt-prone, and it produces disastrous results unless prevented.

The Joy of Guilt-Free Parenting

The power we have been talking about is benevolent power, a power God intended parents to have and use for the good of His children. We know that secular humanists tend to be uncomfortable with anything involving power, but Christians know that power is not only good for the family, it is essential!

With this in mind, we should also be able to see the exercise of parental power in the family as something that honors God. He is love *and* power which He exercises in our lives.

In caring for our children, we can resist the pressure of the world to surrender power and replace it with love. We know good families have *both* love and power, and they do not cancel each other out.

Parent power is a joyous thing for children. Love-based power helps children feel that they will be cared for, cherished, protected, and guided as they grow up. It makes children feel good even when it involves discipline. Parent power ensures the possibility for children to learn the will of God for *their* lives as much as anything else a parent can do.

Parent power without love is destructive!

Guilt-based parent power is often abusive!

Parent love without power is impotent!

We should feel good about getting our power back if we have lost it. We should feel good if we have maintained godly power in the home all along.

The Bible tells us that faith without works is dead (James 2:17). And parenting experience tells us that parenting without power is guilt-laden and dead.

Points for Parents to Ponder

1. Do I wish my spouse understood my perspective on parenting and disciplining?

2. Do I feel there is a "great gulf fixed" between how I was raised and how my spouse was raised?

3. Taking everything as a whole, is our combined parenting style predominately authoritarian?

4. Do I feel at times that I am, in fact, trying to bribe my kids into behaving?

5. When I think of my own childhood, could my feelings be primarily categorized as unhappy or unpleasant?

6. Do my children seem to be playing one parent against the other?

7. The idea of "catch them being good" is a new concept for me.

8. The idea of letting the children have a partial vote in family decisions makes me feel uneasy, although I don't know why.

9. I have felt frustrated at times because our family discipline has often produced other than the best results.

10. I often feel powerless in my parenting.

("Yes" answers indicate tendency to accept the kind of parental guilt discussed in this chapter.)

6 / No Fault, Godly Parenting

Most people have had some experience with visitors to their home whose children seemed largely uncivilized in spite of having very civil parents. The question arises, "How in the world did these parents get such wild children?"

As you would imagine, the answer is complicated, and sometimes uncomfortably close to home.

Linda and I had such an experience a few years back when we were visited by some missionary friends from South America.

Burt and Anna were friends from our very early days as Christians. We had joined the same "Young Marrieds" Sunday School class at about the same time and before either of us had started a family. Not long after that, and before Burt and Anna became parents, they left for a six-year stay in Ecuador. We corresponded by mail and supported them financially along with our church, so we were happy to receive a call from them announcing their arrival back in the States on furlough and wondering if we could get together.

Of course we got together, and we had the unusual opportunity of meeting Billy, five, and four-year-old Susan. That night was one of the longest we have ever spent entertaining guests. The children were absolutely out of control from the moment they entered the house to the moment they left. We only had an infant at that time, but I can recall how stunned we were that *any* children could act so out of control while Mom and Dad sat calmly by, apparently oblivious to the catastrophe that was their children.

They remain friends to this day, and their kids have turned out to be reasonably sound Christian young people, but we are still amazed by the ability of Burt and Anna to be blind to their children's behavior.

Is it really possible to be as unaware as the Jacobsons seemed to be? Or was it simply a defense mechanism of sorts, developed over several years and reflective of their inability to control and discipline their children?

One thing is for sure, there was no sign of the guilty-parent syndrome in this set of parents!

But there are explanations for parental behavior such as we saw in our friends. Some parents have become so shell-shocked by day-by-day behavior of this type and their inability to control it, that they develop the ability not to notice it. Others seem blissfully ignorant of the problems sprouting before their eyes. It's hard to tell if they feel they have found a way to overcome the guilt that afflicts most of us or if they truly just don't notice.

When our children were very young, they went with us to family gatherings, but not much else except church, shopping and such. When it came to visiting in the homes of our friends, babysitters were in order. Looking back on those days, Linda and I reluctantly agree that we were really just unwilling to take the chance that one of our kids might damage something of importance while visiting. We knew that we would have felt guilty and responsible if something had happened. And adding to the guilt was the knowledge that our friends would probably have refused any attempts to replace what was damaged or broken.

We avoided the possibility of guilt and embarrassment by hiring a babysitter.

Holy Spirit led parenting is not no-responsibility parenting. It is the term I have applied to Christian families who allow the Holy Spirit to work in their lives so that they can be the most effective parents they can be. Holy Spirit parenting is not perfect parenting. It is imperfect parenting. But godly Christian parenting is that which allows the Holy Spirit to work in our lives so that we can teach our kids in the way best suited to them.

Holy Spirit parenting relies on the leadership of God in all areas of life, but especially in those areas not specifically spoken to in Scripture—*rather* than relying on someone outside the family to tell us how to raise our children.

Christian parents answer to God both for errors of omission and errors of commission. The challenge is to resist the temptation to avoid any possibility of feeling guilty for the behavior of our offspring by turning to "experts" and trusting them to tell us what to do.

Some of the best parents I have known blame themselves the least when their youngster gets into trouble. Certainly these good parents feel a sense of failure and responsibility when their child fails, but there is a crucial difference between *feeling* responsible and *being* responsible. Parents can experience the emotion without experiencing the reality.

Our oldest child, Laurie, was in junior high school when we discovered she was having trouble telling the truth. We were troubled because Linda and I had always been careful to be truthful with each other and the children. We had reinforced the teachings of God's Word and her Christian school on the subject of truthfulness. Besides that, the things Laurie was lying about were insignificant except for the fact of the lies themselves. If she had told the truth in the first place, nothing major would have resulted.

But because we didn't know how common lying is to young people, we thought we had a major problem on our hands.

As we tried to deal with the lying, we examined ourselves but we were unable to come up with a suitable explanation.

Eventually we realized that Laurie was lying because she was Laurie and thirteen and a sinner just like you and me. Laurie sinned because she was a sinner, *not* because her parents had caused her to lie. We had modeled the right behavior and attitudes for her. We did not lie, and we had taught Laurie and the other children not to lie. In short, though imperfect like all parents, there wasn't a complicated answer. We gave birth to our daughter, and Laurie became as vulnerable to sinning as her parents and every other human being.

Of course we still had to deal with the lying, but we learned that the root of Laurie's sin could be found in her own humanity. This in no way lessened our disappointment in her poor behavior, but our ability to deal with it was not limited by our guilt for what she had done.

Don't misunderstand! We *felt* like blaming ourselves. Most Christian parents feel pain and disappointment (maybe like God did in the Garden of Eden?) when it comes to acknowledging that one of our children could sin. But blaming ourselves would have made it very difficult to see the real cause of Laurie's behavior—her immature understanding of biblical problem-solving coupled with her failure to rely on the Lord Jesus Christ and to live by biblical principles.

Parenting Spirit and Power

As Christian parents, we have many things going for us, most of which are unavailable to parents who do not accept God's Word as truth and as a completely relevant basis for today's living.

God has provided us with all the principles needed to raise children. These principles may be learned through a careful study of the Bible, through reading good books about the Bible, and by hearing the Word taught in worship services and Sunday School. We are *never* without resources for child-rearing.

But, a word of caution. It is important to distinguish principles from specific methods. The Bible is a road map, not a city directory. God intended that we apply His principles where suitable and ask for Holy Spirit guidance when encountering grey areas not specifically addressed in the Bible. This is the essence of "Holy Spirit Parenting."

Principles take precedence over specifics in childrearing because principles apply to *all* children under *all* circumstances, whereas specific examples teach by analogy and may not exactly fit your situation.

Even more important is the fact that the indwelling Holy Spirit will provide every willing parent with access to the truth and guidance for cloudy areas. Every Christian parent has the same equal access to the leadership of the Holy Spirit as any other Christian parent. Christians receive all of the Holy Spirit (a person, don't forget) any of us can receive at the moment of salvation. It remains for us to allow the Holy Spirit to work in our lives.

Parents function at varying levels of efficiency, depending on how open they are to His leading. Parents deeply enmeshed in sin are not going to be open to His leading nor are they going to be as effective with their children as they could and should be. Such parents have the cart before the horse when they ask for Holy Spirit guidance while refusing to deal with sin in their own lives.

Add to this the power of prayer, and it should be easy to see the virtually limitless strength and guilt-free power of a parent living close to the Lord.

As Christian parents, we all need to grow in confidence,

knowing that the prayer of faith is always answered with a yes, a no, or a wait response. If we are sensitive to the leading of the Holy Spirit and if our own lives are in order before God, we can possess a genuine sense of certainty about being able to resolve any family issues.

Godly parenting is spiritual and powerful, but it feels good, too! Only a parent who has gone through deep and troubled waters with a child or teenager can really appreciate the sense of relief that comes with knowing that God is in ultimate charge of our family and our children, and He makes no mistakes.

Age of Responsibility

Being a guilt-free Christian parent requires that we give some thought to the age-old question of personal responsibility in spiritual decisions. When does a person become personally responsible for his or her own actions? What is the age of responsibility? Is there any way parents can know the right time to cut the apron strings of childhood and let the child face God alone?

The answer to all these important questions is a resounding "yes"!

God clearly establishes that each person must answer for his or her own behavior. We read in Proverbs 8:17, "I love them that love me; and those that seek me early shall find me." And again in verse 32 of that same chapter, "Hearken unto me, O ye children: for blessed are they that keep my ways." In Ecclesiastes 12:13-14, God tells us, "Let us hear the conclusion of the whole matter: Fear God, and keep his commandments: for this is the whole duty of man. For God shall bring every work into judgment, with every secret thing, whether it be good, or whether it be evil."

Does God accept young children who come to Him in faith? Certainly He does!

At what age is a young child capable of knowing God?

We don't know the lower limits. But we *do* know that God knows who understands and who does not.

While I was teaching psychology at a Christian college in South Carolina, I became responsible for a Sunday School type visitation at a very large facility for retarded children and teenagers. We taught a simple Bible lesson, played some games, and witnessed where appropriate.

One of the students working with us told me one day that she was afraid the lesson she had tried to teach to her group was above their ability to understand. She was concerned that she hadn't done a very good job in sharing the love of God with these limited youngsters.

I asked her to come by the office the next day to talk about her concerns. In the meantime I talked to another faculty member who had an adult retarded daughter. His answer to my question about the age of accountability shocked me but proved to be just what I needed.

"What do you mean it doesn't matter!" I exclaimed. "How could it not matter?"

He explained that the responsibility for the acceptance and understanding of questions of a moral and spiritual nature does not rest with the one who offers the material. Only the Holy Spirit can prepare a heart to receive the message of salvation, and only the Holy Spirit can direct the response.

He explained that what happens in response lies with the hearer, not the speaker. He suggested that I tell my student to do her best and then pray. The rest is up to God.

What a simple but profound truth that is!

We cannot do God's work for Him. When children are "ready" to accept the message of salvation, they are ready then and not a moment earlier. Parents are only responsible for preparing the way by removing any obstacles that may be in the way of a spiritual decision...including any obstacles in our lives.

93

This is an exact parallel to the problem of guilt we too often experience when one of our kids messes up. As surely as children become Christians in their own time, they will also answer to God individually for their behavior.

Proverbs 22:6

Experience in family counseling teaches many lessons, some easy and pleasant, some difficult. One of the good lessons I have learned concerns the importance of Christian parents in respect to Proverbs 22:6, "Train up a child in the way he should go: and when he is old, he will not depart from it."

What does this verse mean to you?

Proverbs 22:6 is an encouragement to parents. It reminds us that early experiences within the family are influential in later behavior. Some think the verse is more an occupational teaching than a family teaching, referring to the teaching of job-type skills in Bible days when there were no formal schools.

One thing is certain. Proverbs 22:6 affirms that parents are responsible for *preparing* their children for what will come later, not for what those children might actually do when those times arrive!

If Proverbs 22:6 were an actual *guarantee* that parent behavior determines the spiritual destiny of our children, it would mean the following must also be the case:

1. God does have grandchildren, after all! If we can "program" our kids and determine *with certainty* that my children or yours will get saved and lead a good Christian life, then *we* are in control of our children's destiny. They are becoming Christians because of *our* works as parents, rather than the blood of Christ.

2. The work of the Holy Spirit is unnecessary and without effect. Who needs the Holy Spirit if we have Christian parents to bring us to God?

3. Parents are really feeling *less* guilty than we should because we are responsible for *all* the bad behavior of our children, adolescents, and even grown children; we have failed to train them properly, and it *is* our fault after all.

4. God failed as a parent because 100% of His children rebelled and turned away.

Of course these things cannot be true, and as parents we are *not* ultimately responsible for the spiritual position of our grown children. Partially responsible? Of course! Completely responsible? Never!

God knows that some of our children, His children really, are going to reject His Son and the salvation offered. And these decisions to reject will occur independent of anything parents do.

If it were our responsibility to get our youngsters saved, God would have told us so and would have equipped us to do that. He did not, and we are not responsible for the decisions our children ultimately make.

Guilt-Free Godly Parenting

The guilty-parent syndrome usually occurs in Christian families where parents are doing the very best they can under usually less than ideal circumstances. I don't mean to downplay instances where parents have failed badly in their responsibilities. Where this has occurred, parents need t o make it right with God and their family and move forward.

However, most of the guilt I see in Christian parents seems to result from an unrealistic investment in self-blaming, or simply because they have a misbehaving child or teenager and just do not understand the ramifications of that behavior on their family.

Most Christian parents are innocent of most of the charges they have brought against themselves! But they feel responsible and guilty and believe they are *supposed* to accept the blame. Most parents experiencing this syndrome need to apply the truth of the American judicial system to themselves—that people are innocent until proven guilty!

Let me share a personal example with you that may help clarify this issue.

We have missionary friends we have known for more than twenty-five years. They and their four children are as close to us as family.

On their last furlough home, Dan, the father, revealed to me that their oldest son had admitted to homosexuality. He had withdrawn from the Christian college he had been attending and moved to a large city in another part of the country. Although Dan and his wife Betty weren't sure, they believed he was living a totally homosexual lifestyle.

During our many hours of conversation, it became clear to me that Dan had a very strong need to accept the guilt for what his son had done. We worked through the points raised in this book and more, but no amount of biblical input or Christian love could convince this father that the guilt was not his.

Why? Because Dan believed he was required to be the guilt-bearer for the family. The need to feel guilty was also manifested in Dan's need to tell everyone the details of his son's sinful lifestyle.

Dan was not able or willing to come to grips with the truth that any person can choose to do wrong. Dan would rather blame himself and accept that pain than recognize that his son is human and had fallen victim to one of the great sins of this day. Like so many parents, Dan loved his son so much that he had forgotten that he was not God and could not control the destiny of his child.

If Dan's son is truly saved as he proclaims, the Holy Spirit will convict him of the sinful nature of his behavior. We must pray, but conviction, confession, repentance, and correction have to be prompted by the Holy Spirit, not Mom and Dad.

Whose Holy Spirit?

In an attempt to bring all this together, let's consider the role of the Holy Spirit in *each* believer.

No-fault, guilt-free parenting requires that we realize that a child has needs only the Holy Spirit can supply. The Holy Spirit works in both the parents and the misbehaving young person *and* He gives us what we need to deal with problems.

Remember the sleepless summer of seventeen I told you about earlier?

I asked God over and over again to just give Linda and me a break, just a few days of peace and tranquility where we could re-charge our spiritual batteries.

But it didn't happen.

The entire summer was a very rough experience for the Miller family. But what I eventually learned was that Doug needed to experience some things and that the need for him to do so was more important to the Holy Spirit than our peace of mind as parents.

You may be suffering right now as Linda and I did a few summers ago. But be confident. The Spirit who works in us is also working in the hearts of our youngsters for their benefit. The days and nights may seem long and troubled, and the pain and sense of loss can be powerful. But as we suffer, our children learn and grow.

We may have to suffer for their good, but we should not feel guilty, too!

Points for Parents to Ponder

1. Do you often try to "tune out" the children?

2. Are you, as Linda and I were, reluctant to take the kids with you when visiting?

3. Do you rely on "experts" to tell you how to raise your children?

4. Do you often feel that if you were a better parent, your children would be better, too?

5. Do you often feel that God has abandoned you in your child-rearing responsibilities?

6. Do you believe that there is a set "age of responsibility"?

7. Do you take Proverbs 22:6 as a guarantee from God that children raised right will turn out right?

8. Like my friend Dan, whose son admitted to living as a homosexual, do you feel guilty for your child's sins?

9. Do you find yourself asking God for a "break" from parenting, as Linda and I did?

10. Do you feel that other parents have more spiritual understanding than you?

("Yes" answers indicate tendency to accept the kind of parental guilt discussed in this chapter.)

7 / Discipline and Attitudes

Guilt-free Christian parenting is built on a foundation of self-confidence and fortified with the experiences of one's own childhood. Not only do we parent as we were parented, but we tend to live out the roles imposed on us by our parents. Those of us afflicted with parental guilt, fostered not by our own behavior but by that of a child or adolescent, are living out the roles we learned when we were children.

If we feel responsible when a child brings home a poor report card and the teacher comments that incomplete homework was a contributor to the poor showing, it is because we were raised by a parent or parents who taught us by their actions that if a child fails to do well in school, there must be something wrong with that child's parents.

Many of us spend the greater part of our lives fulfilling prophecies of our parents and then feeling guilty either because we *did* what our parents expected us to do (fail, for example) or because we did *not* do what our parents expected of us (succeed, go to college, for example).

Let me share a very personal story about myself and my family that might help to clarify this point.

My family is a working class group of people centered in Detroit. Every relative I knew by name, and it seemed as if there were hundreds, lived within walking distance of where I lived as I grew up. There was a lot of security in this kind of a neighborhood, and I remember having a very happy childhood.

All my male relatives, and many female relatives as well, worked either in the automobile plants or steel mills. My family, my neighborhood, my school, virtually everything about my life was "blue-collar." And I liked it that way!

But I began to wonder if maybe my high school counselor was wrong when he suggested to me that my future probably would be found in the factories of Detroit, just like all my relatives to that point.

I accepted this flawed bit of advice, stayed with a "general" program in high school, and went to work at Great Lakes Steel Corporation in Ecorse, Michigan, immediately after graduating from high school. Linda and I married in 1961, Laurie was born in 1963, and I was not-so-happily toiling away in one of the factories predicted by my high school "guidance" counselor.

But I once again began to wonder if this was what I was supposed to be doing. Linda and I, along with her parents had been saved in the fall of 1961, and I was beginning to wonder if God had something different in store for me.

So I enrolled in a junior college, took two classes, and got D's in both, still living up to the expectations of my parents (get an honest job) and my high school counselor (your future lies in factory work of some kind). I did poorly in those first two classes because I was living up to expectations that had been ingrained in me over the years by many different people. I was so convinced that I was not college material that I dropped out.

But thanks to Linda (who got straight A's all the way through school) and some good teaching at my new church on the idea that we can do all things through Christ, I re-enrolled, eventually transferred to Wayne State University for a four-year program, graduated, and became a teacher. It's a long story, but the point I need to make is very brief. During all those years when I was pursuing an education, including a master's degree, and eventually a Ph.D., I habitually found myself sort of *apologizing* to my parents for going on with my schooling. I used to think I did this so they would not feel that I was being arrogant with my education, but now I think I was apologizing for *contradicting their expectations of me!*

I was taught as a child that honest people work with their hands and that too much education was a dangerous thing. My uncles used to tease me as a young husband and father about when was I going to grow up and quit going to school.

As a result of this, I felt the need to apologize for my "radical" behavior to my family.

This was always done in a lighthearted, joking kind of way. My family has always been very nice to one another, but the message got through. And even today as I approach fifty years of age, when I am in the presence of one of my uncles or my father, I feel a need to downplay what is going on in my life. I am not, after all, living up to their expectations for me!

What kind of expectations did your parents have for you as you were growing up? Is there some confusion in your life right now, as there was in mine, about why you feel the way you do or why you react as you do? As we consider the following aspects of parenting, let's remind ourselves of how much we are influenced by those childhood teachings.

Optimal Attitude
Effective, guilt-free parents who practice sound disciplinary

101

techniques seem to share an attitude about discipline that is distinctive. This attitude is a wonderful thing to behold and creates a sense of awe in those of us who don't seem to have it.

Principals look for it when hiring new teachers. Counselors hope to find it or develop it when working with parents. It's always missing in families of *chronically* delinquent youngsters and adult criminals. It is that magic element judges and social case workers say cannot be created if it is missing.

The optimal attitude is composed of more or less equal parts confidence and competence, two elements essential in disciplining *and* leading children and adolescents. When found in adults, it always repeats itself in the lives of the young people they touch. The optimal attitude crosses generational boundaries.

Though somewhat mysterious and hard to pin down, we know that children raised by parents who possess the optimal attitude are benefited by it and pass it along to their own children.

Let's look at how this optimal attitude shows itself in parenting.

The Optimal Attitude in Action

Guilt-free discipline and guilt-free parenting result from a mental attitude. It involves a high level of quiet, controlled confidence that is almost always based in some measure on a felt calling from God that, "This is what I am supposed to be doing and I trust that God would not have given me these children to raise if He didn't trust me to do a good job."

Trust in God is important to the kind of child-rearing we are discussing here because righteous trust can significantly reduce the amount of felt guilt in any parent. "God and I make a majority" we say, and confident parents *really* believe it! The simple confidence that we are not alone in our parenting efforts is of great help. Our awareness of God's presence through the Holy Spirit during dark times can be *the* single thing that pulls us through.

All stressed parents, and that's just about all of us at some time or other, learn that God is holding on to us; it's not we who are holding on to Him.

This parental attitude of confidence about child-rearing will help youngsters behave even when Mom and Dad are not around. My principal at Wilson Junior High School in Detroit explained early on in my teaching experience that a good teacher is known for what happens when he or she *leaves* the room more than what goes on when he is there with the kids. Children and teens easily pick up the messages their parents send out—good or bad—and learn to structure their behavior around those messages.

An optimal parental attitude is more of a controlling element in families raising children and teens than anything else. It includes values, behaviors, spiritual teaching, political viewpoints—just anything we can think of. Such attitudes of confidence and power under God are sensed by children very early in life, often before their long-term memory is functioning. That is why most of us cannot remember how we learned what we learned from Mom and Dad.

Christian parents have an added advantage, of course. We have the knowledge that we can do all things through Christ and that we can come boldly before His throne for help in time of need (Hebrews 4:16). His grace and power are ours for the asking. This "optimal attitude" for Christians will help eliminate many problems before they have a chance to develop.

Attitudes in Children and Teens

Children and teens want limits on their behavior. In the midst of strong objections to the placement and enforcement of limits, young people nevertheless receive a healthy dose of security from them. Parents cannot be reticent about dispensing such preventative "medications" when their youngsters need them.

The point is that kids want help staying out of trouble even though very few can put this need into words. I have counseled many young people in trouble for everything from poor grades in school to unwed pregnancies and drug addiction. I have counseled adolescents on the verge of being removed from their home and placed in a detention facility. But past all toughness and anger, past all resentment and feelings of abuse, they have a deep sense of despair because they feel that their parents don't love them.

How could they feel this way when Mom is in the outer courtroom crying her eyes out and Dad has spent thousands of dollars on lawyers trying to keep a son or daughter out of trouble?

How could they feel this way in the face of all the evidence that Mom and Dad *do* care?

Because, as they tell me, "If Mom and Dad had *really* cared about me, they would have taken the trouble to say 'no' when I needed them to." In their heart of hearts, these kids are disappointed with their parents for letting them get into trouble too easily, and they are frightened—not by judicial punishment—but at the perception that their parents don't love them enough to discipline them and maybe keep them *out* of trouble.

Yes, there are kids who are going to get into trouble in spite of having the best parents God ever made. But most are not in that category. Most of the troubled kids I come across have been *allowed* to get into trouble because Mom and Dad were more interested in temporary happiness or temp-orary convenience than in what was best for their children in the long run. These kids are almost always scared to death…by the realization that they are on their own. Mom and Dad abdicated their responsibility to someone else.

Kids of all ages feel better and *are* better when they have parents who have the will power to tell them "no."

Not too long ago I faced a situation that is a good example of what I mean.

Josh was thirteen when I met him. He had been brought in by his mom and dad in spite of my request that I see them alone for the first session. I think they just didn't want to leave him home with his brothers.

Josh was average size, bright-looking with clear brown eyes that seemed to notice everything, well-dressed but kind of "teenage radical." The youngest of three boys, this was a kid from a good Christian family who had decided to get away with anything he could.

Josh's parents had asked to see me because their son's behavior was deteriorating rapidly, and they were at a loss to explain why. Their parenting had been successful with Josh's older brothers, so why was Josh "going crazy" on them?

As their story unfolded, I saw a pattern emerging. Josh was feeling a need to "push the envelope" of family rules he had lived with all his life. I felt that Josh was asking, in the only way possible for him, for Mom and Dad to show some strength, to step in and help him say "no" to those things that were getting him into such serious trouble. Josh was determined to continue being bad until someone, maybe even his parents, said "enough is enough" and forced him to behave. I believed, and I shared this with his parents, that once he was reassured that he was loved enough to be protected even from himself, the unacceptable behavior would stop.

So what was the problem?

Aren't parents genetically programmed to say "no"?

Well, not Josh's parents. And both were in tears during our first session because of their frustration and anger. They didn't understand why their previously successful, biblically based methods of childrearing had suddenly failed.

But what had worked with the older boys was a permissive,

loose, loving, and friendly home atmosphere where things were just kind of accepted unless they were totally out of line.

What Josh's parents had to realize was that they had to alter their parenting practices somewhat in order to meet the special needs represented by *this* thirteen-year-old.

Would Josh's grandfather have put up with such behavior from Josh's dad when he was younger?

"Absolutely not," was the quick reply.

"What, then, is the difference?" I asked.

"But Josh is different," they replied, almost simultaneously. "Josh is different from the other boys and from his dad when he was a boy."

"Exactly my point," I said. "So why would you want to continue dealing with Josh in such a way that makes him feel you don't love him just because it worked with the older boys?"

Josh had picked up the signals of weak parenting and had chosen to exploit them. Josh's attitude was a *direct* result of his parents' attitude, particularly his father's.

Parental attitude controls child attitude.

After many sessions with Josh and other sessions with his parents, things improved. But they improved *only* when his dad accepted my challenge to toughen up with his son and see what happened.

And what happened pleased them. Sure enough, Josh straightened up. Josh explained his better behavior by claiming that he now "had to behave" because "my dad won't put up with it anymore."

Josh found the symbols of love he was looking for, and once he found them, he became a relatively normal kid again.

Attitude is everything with teenagers. Not only their attitude, but the attitude of their parents as well. One of the hardest lessons Linda and I had to learn was that *our* attitude needed to change to meet the changing needs of our children as they became teenagers. Once that lesson "took," things began to improve with the Miller family just as it did with Josh and his parents.

Personal History

Each of us has our own history of being a child, and part of that history, a very important part for some of us, relates to how we were disciplined by our parents.

We learn to be parents by being children, and we learn to be disciplinarians by being disciplined. To rephrase that popular axiom, what goes around in parenting really *does* come around later.

But this is not family predestination we are talking about. It is just a statement about family living that acknowledges the crucial importance of our personal history of childhood. This is not predestination because we have the power to break the chain if need be and put a new pattern of parent behavior in its place.

But along with the opportunity comes the responsibility!

Most of us were raised by parents who did a pretty good job with us. Now here we are, grown up and trying our best to live right and take care of our families. Our parents must have done well, or we wouldn't have turned out as good as we did. Just go ahead and pat yourself on the back if you feel like it. I won't tell!

It is possible that our parents did, in fact, do a very good job of parenting us. Of course, we were not kids in the nineties. We were kids in the seventies, sixties, or fifties, or forties, and *we* didn't have to face the kind of problems *our* kids are facing today, did we? It is equally possible that some of their methods are not appropriate to deal with the situations of the nineties.

Our *parents* didn't have to face all the problems of the nineties when they were raising us.

What we know for sure is that flexibility and a strong sense

107

of purpose is required, yes, required, if children and teens are going to be effectively parented today. As Christians, we are not talking about compromising Bible doctrine or principle, but, rather, being able to be flexible with those matters of life unrelated to doctrine, especially in matters of method.

Statistics tell us that about one person in five will have been physically or sexually abused as a child. Because we learn how to discipline from being disciplined, and at a very early age as well, when we find ourselves in a stressful situation as an adult, we tend to regress and do what was done to us, including being abusive in discipline. If we had bad parenting or were abused or abandoned, we will have the tendency to repeat that pattern in our families. Only when we are aware of those tendencies can we successfully fight against making the mistakes of our parents.

It is strange indeed that people should repeat the abusive behaviors of their parents when they were so unpleasant in the first place. What we need to understand is that children fear abandonment more than anything else and abuse by a parent raises the specter of potential abandonment.

Abuse tells children they are worthless and at risk for being removed from the family. Children instinctively react to that fear by "bonding" with the abuser in hopes that they will not be abandoned. "See, I'm still your friend even though you hurt me" goes the subconscious reasoning of the child. "And if I let you hurt me, you will still be my parent. Right?"

Our childhood experiences do repeat themselves in our adult behaviors as parents.

Inconsistent Discipline Patterns

The cycle of inconsistent discipline, the resultant parental guilt feelings, then a need to convince self and others that we are not really lenient, followed by harshness followed by guilt is a process that may *never* end. Someone has to break the chain so that our kids don't grow up thinking that's how *they* should parent.

So how do you decide if your discipline is inconsistent?

We may fail to impose reasonable restrictions, boundaries really, in the home. Or, the limitations and rules may be imposed in one situation and not another, or on one child and not the others. We may do one thing today and another thing tomorrow.

Even though inconsistent parents often threaten to punish, they follow through only sporadically on their words. Parents, teachers, anyone working with young people should know the danger in making threats that cannot or will not be backed up with action.

Some have developed the practice of apologizing after disciplining children or teens. This is perhaps one of the clearest signs of the guilty-parent syndrome. Why would a parent apologize for disciplining a child *unless* that parent wasn't sure the action required discipline. If we are not sure, we should not discipline. I see this often even in Christian families who know all the biblical information on the need to discipline ourselves and our youngsters, yet many suffer the effects of their need to apologize for what they claim was the right thing to do. I have never understood why, when a Christian parent knows the disciplinary action is right, they apologize. It tells the child that the discipline is wrong. When we apologize for doing right, it sends very confusing signals to an immature mind. Parenting is a serious business we have agreed to do for God. We should not apologize for "tough love" actions.

Inconsistent parents typically have ambivalent feelings about their children and about their suitability for parenting. A blessing from God the children may be, but parents wonder why they are blessed with a learning disabled child, a retarded child, a hyperactive child, a child with an uncooperative spirit, or any of the other hundreds of conditions that can make parenting a real challenge. All parents experience ambivalence at some time or another. Inconsistent parents feel it *most* of the time.

Inconsistency also produces a compulsion in parents to explain the reasons behind the rules when children question the parent's authority. There is nothing wrong with explaining before administering discipline. What *is* a problem is the parent who feels that he or she *must* explain and that the child *must* understand and agree with the reason for discipline. This always results in weakened discipline in the home. Remember, parents do not owe their children or teenagers an explanation!

If a parent wishes to explain, fine! But there should not be the feeling of being forced or compelled to explain. Giving reasons for everything a parent does sets up expectations in a young person that this is the normal course of events. It teaches that the youngster *deserves* an explanation, and this is not the case. The demand for explanations will overlap onto other areas and the parent will find more and more energy going to persuading the young person to do what they should do. Parents often act correctly based only on intuition, and intuition cannot be explained to anyone!

Inconsistent parents will also be very sensitive to accusations of not loving the child or teenager. "If you loved me, you would let me go to that party." Believe it or not, some of us fall for this, especially from adolescents! Because some of us question our ability to parent effectively, we are vulnerable to all kinds of accusations, not only from our own children and teens, but also from the media or people at church. In turn, as parents, we feel a need to justify ourselves by explaining.

Parents sometimes respond to these accusations with a declaration of love usually followed by permission to do what was once forbidden—and all motivated by parent guilt! Inconsistent parents, for whatever reasons and in whatever form, tell their youngsters that they are ambivalent toward them. This leads to greater misbehavior as the kids feel less and less secure. Giving in and overindulgence are clear symptoms of this kind of problem.

The results of inconsistent discipline patterns are evidenced in children and teens by serious and negative behavior such as:

1. Nightmares and other sleep disturbances. (Inconsistency in parents threatens the security of the children.)
2. Non-compliance with parental commands.
3. Temper tantrums.
4. Increased sibling rivalry and bickering.
5. Stealing.
6. Aggressive behavior, including bullying younger or smaller children.
7. Truancy and other forms of school-based misbehavior.
8. Restlessness and excitability.

These behaviors are an attempt to provoke parents or others into imposing increased limitations on them so their sense of security will be enhanced. This really isn't so complicated! Remember, kids want someone who cares enough to control their behavior, not give in to it. All we have to do is back up and try to imagine what the situation feels like to the five, ten, or fifteen-year-old...even though he won't know why he is misbehaving.

The Overuse of Discipline

One of the greatest lessons I have learned through several years of counseling is that moderation can prevent and solve a multitude of problems. The key to dealing with teenagers is negotiation, and we are beginning to realize that even with children, a willingness to listen to their side of the story "softens" many problems.

While some parents resort to leniency to bribe their youngsters into obedience, others become legalistic and harsh.

111

They overuse discipline and punishment. When we use excessively harsh, too frequent, or thoughtless discipline, we can be sure of at least two things: One, that we are doing so out of a spirit of fear, and second, that it won't be effective in controlling the misbehavior for very long.

One of the truisms of life is that we try to control those things that most frighten us. Very harsh parents *are always* the most frightened, least self-confident, and least effective parents in the neighborhood. Eventually, youngsters always react to excessive discipline with increased bad behavior, sensing their parents' uncertainty about being parents.

Let's discuss some of the predictable side-effects of an over-reliance on harsh methods of child and adolescent discipline.

First of all, let's define overuse. The idea involves more frequent than average use of physical or other methods of child control designed primarily to *coerce* children and teens into compliance with parental demands. At the same time, this parent sees punishment, particularly corporal punishment, as a parent's *first* response to misbehavior rather than the *last*!

Perhaps a couple of examples will help make the point.

As I mentioned earlier, Linda and I have been privileged to be members of four really excellent independent fundamental churches in the nearly thirty years we have been Christians. In each church, our pastor was reasonable and very biblical on all matters including family concerns. But occasionally a visiting preacher or evangelist made comments that struck us as less than reasonable and "extra-biblical."

I recall one older evangelist visiting our church in Michigan to speak on the subject of the family.

At one point, this older, well-known preacher took questions from the congregation.

A young father stood up and asked, "Dr. _____, how old should a child be before we begin spanking?"

112

"How old is your child?" the preacher asked.

"About six months. He's just a baby."

"Well, you're six months too late!" the man responded. Keep in mind that this evangelist was in his late seventies at the time and was recognized as an authority on the Christian family. He had written dozens of books on the subject for the Christian audience. I do not know how seriously the congregation took his comments, but he was *not* kidding!

I hesitate to use the next example because when I tell people about it, I get the feeling that I am not believed. Surely, no one could have really said what I am about to tell you. But he did!

Again, this was a visiting speaker on the family about fifteen years after the first example. The subject of child discipline came up in a question and answer time, and this Christian man proclaimed his belief that *children should be spanked every day because they have certainly done things that would deserve a spanking and gotten away with them, and so that they do not get the idea that sin can be gotten away with, they should be spanked even if you don't know for sure what they did!*

Am I kidding?

I only wish I were because this man is still out there speaking in churches and unknowingly recommending the destruction of the Christian family.

These examples are pretty extreme, I'll agree, but they do illustrate the idea of what I mean by excessive and overly harsh discipline. Not only do children suffer when discipline is over-used, but parents suffer as well. Guilt is a natural by-product of excessive and harsh discipline. And if we are taught that such extreme methods are biblical, as is often the case, there is even more guilt and ambivalence when we see we are offending our children if we do and supposedly offending God if we don't.

Excessive discipline *will* create harmful side effects. Anxiety created by the fear of the pain or rejection caused by harsh methods may lead the child to fear the *parent* more than the misbehavior. Many children have become "flinchy" around *all* adults because they are forever getting hit at home. Parents who are the primary source of love and security become the primary source of pain and unhappiness in these families, leading to great psychological and spiritual damage such as serious anxiety or depression. This is a "double-bind" situation that can absolutely destroy children. Teenagers will just run away.

Another side effect is that parental violence (and spanking by any other name *is* violent) supplies a model of aggressive behavior for the child to emulate. This seems especially powerful in boys, the more naturally aggressive sex. Even though a harsh, physically punitive dad will have well-controlled children, the teenagers in the family will rise up and say good-bye.

The approach will create some major discipline problems when the boys become too big to threaten. Boys will also tend to carry the aggression into adulthood, providing a major explanation for the fact that child abuse and wife-beating tends to run in families.

In addition, harsh methods may set up escape behaviors even more dangerous than the child's offense. Typically, such children are at risk for running away or lying to escape being punished. If children know they will be beaten when they bring that bad report card home, their motivation for trying to change the grade is magnified. Perhaps they will forge the parent's signature rather than bring the card home. In fact, children can be so frightened of the anticipated beating they are going to receive that they will do almost anything, even suicide at times, to escape it.

Harsh methods can be expected to create more problems than they solve.

And what happens when the child becomes "hardened" to the punishment?

Most of us would think that it is impossible to become "used to" being hit by a parent. But there are countless children and young people out there who have been able to "numb out" when Mom or Dad starts beating on them. This may not be common in your experience or mine, but it is a reality for many thousands of American youngsters.

While they have found a way to deal with the physical pain, their sense of rejection is another matter. Feeling rejected brings along feelings of being unloved and unlovable, worthless, ugly, and embarrassed. These feelings are not so easy to shrug off.

Punishment is like many other things: Too much of anything is likely to reach a saturation point so that eventually no reaction is visible. I have seen teens who had become so hardened against an over-controlling father who beat them that they challenged their fathers to try to make them cry or react to the pain they were feeling.

This same kind of defiance may occur to a lesser degree in families where punishment is too heavily relied on, although no abuse could be charged.

Have you ever wondered how prostitutes, drug addicts and bums can live in such squalid conditions and abuse their bodies so badly? Without seeming to care about what happens to them?

That's right. These are probably the adult results of children who were taught that they are worthless, ugly, unlovable, and so on. The messages we receive in childhood *never* leave us.

Are there *any* positive results from excessive or harsh discipline?

Such methods *will* stop the unwanted behavior for a time. Spanking a child today for sassing Mom will probably assure that he or she will not talk back to Mom today, but it does not guarantee what will happen tomorrow or when Mom is not around. For an unwanted behavior to be eliminated in the future, the motivation for misbehaving must be understood, dealt with, and altered. This cannot be accomplished with physical methods alone.

Physical discipline can be effective if used moderately, in love, and in *combination* with other, less painful controls. If physical discipline is relied on exclusively, though, strong negative side-effects of the type we have been discussing are guaranteed.

If we are going to use spanking or some other physical method for child discipline, the well-being of the child must be uppermost in the mind of the parent. Retribution and revenge have no place in a Christian's child discipline. Nor should spanking or other physical methods ever be used on teenagers. There is no biblical permission for it.

Avoidance of Guilt in Disciplining

We hear a great deal these days about child abuse. And with good reason! But trying to find out what *really* goes on in good and bad families is difficult. We do know that there is a relationship between good discipline and good parenting, and we also know that one cannot exist without the other.

What follows is an informal report on what research has found on the subject of child discipline. I emphasize research because I want you to know that these ideas are based on *scientifically* valid fact-based investigations. *All* the findings are thoroughly and completely consistent with biblical teaching on the subject. Where there might be disagreement, look to someone's *interpretation* of either science or the Bible to find out why.

Good discipline is consistent and moderate. The methods are applied in approximately the same manner each time a similar offense is committed by the same child. Such parental consistency leads to security, a sense of unconditional love and acceptance, and self-confidence in both parent and child.

Good discipline also provides a child with warning signals, usually verbal, before the discipline is administered. Children can really benefit from a quick, "Watch it!" when they come too close to the boundary separating acceptable behavior from unacceptable behavior. Warning signals also reduce parental guilt because the parents know they have done everything reasonable to discourage the unwanted behavior.

Good discipline is administered almost immediately after the misbehavior, but after Mom and Dad has calmed down. Once the anger has subsided, we should get the discipline over with as quickly as possible. There is simply no biblical or other reason to justify a prolonged waiting period for children. The shorter the time between an act and its consequences, the better the learning. And either parent can administer discipline. There is no need to wait until Dad gets home.

Good discipline includes the removal of privileges such as television time or play opportunities combined with more physical methods such as a spanking. The methods for restoration of privileges should be spelled out ahead of time and in a way the child can understand.

And finally, good discipline pays attention to good behavior as well as bad. Unwanted behavior may be eliminated if parents choose to *ignore* it and concentrate on reinforcing the good behavior. In this sense, *good* discipline is flexible as it looks at *all* the behaviors of the child, good, bad, and indifferent!

Developing Guilt-Free Discipline

In families with parents who have avoided most major mistakes like divorce, abuse, and addictions, disciplinary methods provide the next most fertile ground for the development of parental guilt.

The major way to avoid guilt is to develop the proper

attitude about children, parenting, and discipline. This brings us back to square one.

When parents claim their right to do whatever is necessary within the laws of God and man to make it difficult for our child or teenager to do wrong, we are on the way to guilt-free discipline. When we make good on our promise to God to raise our kids in the nurture and admonition of the Lord, we are farther along our way to guilt-free discipline.

Once we have developed this mindset, we will have come to grips with the fundamental idea that both parents and children have certain inalienable rights within the family and that the development and actualization of these rights leads to a healthy family.

Guilt-free discipline can be achieved for a very small price. The cost is nothing more than Mom and Dad's commitment *to obey God* in disciplining children, *to understand* what God does tell us to do, *and to know* what He is silent about.

Benefits of Guilt-Free Discipline

The benefits of guilt-free discipline ought to be obvious by now. We will feel better about ourselves and our kids, worry less about making mistakes, be less anxious, be less embarrassed when something goes wrong, and walk closer to the Lord by doing what God wants us to do. There will also be fewer arguments between parents and kids; the home will be less chaotic; the family will have more fun being with each other.

Children will see it a little differently because they may experience some strange and new attitudes in Mom and Dad that may take some getting used to. But they will eventually learn that Mom and Dad can't be bullied anymore. They will discover that Mom and Dad aren't as vulnerable to threats, whining, and pestering. Even temper tantrums no longer do their expected job of upsetting Mom and Dad and making them give in to whatever the child wants. They will sense that their parents know how to handle family situations, and there will be fewer challenges to Mom and Dad's authority and responsibilities.

There are other benefits as well. The major one is a strong sense of confidence by children in those same parents they used to manipulate. Kids will become calmer, less argumentative, and more secure. Children raised by guilt-free parents develop high levels of self-esteem, good social skills, and an optimistic outlook on their own future marriages. They sense that their parents know how to handle family difficulties with good parenting methods. They will, in turn, pass them on to their children.

It circles back to the major idea discussed at the first of the chapter: Parent attitude controls child attitude.

Guilt-free parenting is what God would have us practice; it is what He uses with us when we misbehave, and eventually even my children and yours will rise up and call us blessed!

Points for Parents to Ponder

1. Do you believe your parents felt guilty when they were raising you?

2. Are you fulfilling the "prophecies" of your parents?

3. Are you fulfilling the prophecies of others for you?

4. Do you feel like apologizing to your parents for your life?

5. Are you missing out on the "optimal attitude"?

6. Is it hard for you to tell your children "no"? Do you give in when they beg for something you said "no" to?

7. Does the story of Josh remind you of one or more of your own teenagers?

8. Do you feel the way you were parented has limited your ability to be an effective parent?

9. Were you physically, sexually, or emotionally abused as a child?

10. Do you apologize to your children or teens after they have been disciplined?

("Yes" answers indicate tendency to accept the kind of parental guilt discussed in this chapter.)

8 / Recognizing Family Patterns

Catherine Jamison was forty-two going on thirteen when I first saw her for counseling. She was depressed, anxious, dependent on others to an unusual extent, and bitterly unhappy in her marriage. I had the very strong feeling that Catherine was telling me that if something didn't happen soon to change her feelings, she would resort to something drastic for escape.

I quickly realized that Catherine was an adult victim of parental alcoholism and divorce, and she was emotionally "stuck" at age thirteen, her age when the family system finally collapsed. Even now, so many years later, Catherine could not tell me the most obvious facts about her childhood without bursting into tears and heart-wrenching sobs.

Catherine slowly became able to share some of the more powerful experiences of her youth: the time her three-year-old brother stood crying on the front porch because their alcoholic and recently divorced father "forgot" to come and pick him up for the day, or the time her father had come home in a drunken stupor and stumbled into Catherine's bedroom thinking it was his. Though no sexual abuse actually occurred, the memory of this near miss was so powerful that it took many months before Catherine could share it with me.

Many sad or frightening experiences still played on Catherine's mind, even thirty years later.

Catherine's mother had leaned more and more on her young teenage daughter after the divorce. Catherine became her little brother's "other mom" as he called her sometimes. Cathy took on a lot of responsibility for her little brother, missing her exams at the end of her junior year in high school because he was ill and someone had to stay home with him.

Her mother relied heavily on her to take care of the family bills, also. Later, Catherine was able to trace her anxiety about money to that responsibility which was too much for her young shoulders to carry. She loved her mother and sought to please her. But often her mother became disgusted. "You're just like your father!" she repeated over and over. For the longest time Cathy was afraid she would end up a nymphomaniac if she wasn't careful; her father had been unfaithful to her mother for years with partner after partner.

She also feared alcohol. Her father's heavy drinking was a source of many problems in the home. What if she touched alcohol and became an alcoholic—just like her father?

But she loved her father and felt guilty, on one hand, and resentful, on the other, because he had left them. Talking with a young girl whose father had recently died, she reminded the girl that at least her father hadn't wanted to go away and leave her. Her father had. She was thirty when she realized that the bitterness she carried was only hurting one person—herself.

Catherine had strong, mixed feelings about both her parents. She knew that her mother despised her father's drinking, but she was confused as to why her mother put up with it for so long. And her father, well, total confusion reigned when it came to him.

Catherine said she loved her father but felt guilty somehow for causing the divorce. This, in spite of the fact that the marriage had been doomed for several years and her mother had told her over and over again that she and her brother had nothing to do with the break-up.

What was almost obvious with Catherine was that she was suffering as an adult because of being raised as a child in a dysfunctional home. She and her little brother were the victims of extremely poor parenting which was *allowed* to occur over the years of her growing up.

Catherine needed to understand that she was still carrying her mother's burden for her just as she had as a young girl, and it was time to put down the load. What Catherine needed and received in counseling was awareness of why she was still feeling so badly and what needed to happen if she was ever going to be able to put her past behind her and move into adulthood completely.

The Need for Self-Awareness

There are many ways self-awareness can be defined. Probably most would agree that being self-aware means knowing yourself better than others know you.

The presence or absence of self-awareness is more a function of early learning than anything else. Just as good or poor parenting tends to be inherited and passed from one generation to the next, self-awareness is usually a result of the quality of parenting we experience. There are exceptions, and many folks have been able to rise above their upbringing, but the need for parental self-awareness stems from this very real transmission of traits to the children. Good parenting runs in families and produces generation after generation of people who have stable marriages, are non-abusive to their children, contribute to the community, practice a carefully thought-through faith, and focus more on others than on themselves.

But poor parenting runs in families, too, and results in generational patterns of child and spousal abuse, alcoholism and other addictions, obesity, and even criminality. Opportunities for changing deviant family patterns, those most likely to both result from and cause parental guilt, are usually limited to the years before we have children or when the children are very small. Parents often lose their willingness to learn and to change very quickly after beginning a family.

If changes are to be made, we must be exposed to correct parenting practices in the early years of our marriage. It's not that older parents cannot change; it is simply more difficult. I have worked with hundreds of middle-aged parents, for example, who *were* able to change some important aspect of their parenting. Along with the desire and willingness to change must also go an understanding of how we arrived where we are and how personal traits may be causing problems in the family. This is a big order.

Let's look at some situations most likely to lead to parental guilt. As we think more deeply about our family and the family of our youth, we will see how we are being affected by both now. Think about the following questions and answer them about your present family.

Family Environment
1. Does the family make enough money collectively to meet most of their important needs?
2. Do husband and wife seem happy with their occupations?
3. Is the family happy with its geographic location and type and condition of housing?
4. Does the family consistently practice a religious belief?
5. Do family members socialize on a regular basis with people other than family?

Each "no" answer for these questions represents a potential problem capable of evolving into a major crisis.

Remember, this quiz is designed to encourage us to be more self-aware.

Family Health

1. Are family members in good health?
2. If some members are in poor health, how is this impacting the other family members?
3. Does the family have the resources to adjust to this illness?

Nothing impacts the psychological and spiritual well-being of a family like a chronic illness. Take a few moments to consider how you might deal with these situations should they arise.

Family Emotional Condition

1. Do family members communicate their emotions openly and honestly with each other, or are emotions hidden and "out of bounds"?
2. Has emotional bonding taken place between different generations of the family?
3. Is negotiation possible when disagreements arise, or do such clashes typically conclude with an autocratic decision by someone?
4. Is there emotional strength in the family, and does the family recognize these strengths?
5. Do secrets exist which cannot be discussed?

My family is probably less emotionally expressive than most. My family background is Eastern European and Linda's is one hundred percent British. Both of our families are conservative about emotional expression. Your family is probably different from ours and even from your friends. I am not proposing one variety is superior to another. What *does* make a difference, though, is awareness of what the emotional tone of the family is and how it may be impacting individual members. It is the "unspeakable" nature of emotions in some families that can lead to trouble.

Family Role Division

1. Is there a clear understanding of the different roles and functions of the various family members?
2. Is there an understood and accepted division of labor?
3. Is one or more of the children expected to act as substitute parent at times?
4. Are parents in agreement about family discipline?
5. Is there an obvious role conflict between parents?

Blurred boundaries, especially those that cross generational lines, are a major source of family problems: Older children taking Mom's place while she works or is ill; an older son trying to replace Dad after the divorce; daughters becoming "stand in wives" for Dad while Mom is away or ill. Sound extreme? Talk to a family counselor and see how often these problems surface even in Christian families. Clear, agreed upon boundaries that do not cross generational lines are necessary for family health.

Family Structure

1. Who holds most of the power in the family?
2. Do family members go their own way rather than live as a unit?
3. Are family members restricted from becoming involved in outside activities or from becoming too close to someone outside the family?
4. Are family activities designed to meet the needs of *all* members of the family or just the parents?
5. Does the family have to do all its activities together?

6. Are family members over-involved (enmeshed) in each other's lives?

The family unit was originated and designed by God to do two things: raise children in the nurture and admonition of His Word *and* release them into the world mature and capable of doing His will. Enmeshment or over-involvement always seems to result in parents being unwilling to let their children grow up to be independent of them. The family is supposed to be fluid and flexible rather than rigid and unchangeable. The best measure of the job Christian parents have done is what the grown children do as adults on their own. Parental attempts to keep children from becoming independent are doomed to fail and will likely cause an eventual breach in the family emotional bond.

You and I must be able to assess our own family structure on a regular basis and be prepared to help those who are not doing so. What I have suggested above is not etched in stone. They are simply ideas designed to prompt each us of to think about what we are doing as parents.

Guilt Producers

Once we have made our collective ways through the self-awareness signposts, we can turn to a more detailed analysis of the sources of individual guilt in parents. The goal of this section is to enable each of us to become stronger through the development of clearer perceptions of family responsibility. Counselors and therapists are fond of reminding young people considering marriage that, "You can't give yourself to another until you have a self to give." Parents deal with this issue as well, though in a very different form.

Christians have power from God and the Holy Spirit to correct anything that needs correcting and to change what demands changing, but it is no surprise to any of us that most

127

people *do not change* what needs changing even after becoming a Christian. God doesn't fail us, but His offer of help is not believed or accepted, and no change occurs.

Many of us carry some measure of "incompleteness" from our childhood and that sense of being less than we should as adults makes it very difficult to be what we should be as parents.

Did you do the self-evaluation above? If you did, we can look at how these and other family patterns lead to guilt-producing problems. Parents become better able to defend themselves against parental guilt when they are more aware of guilt-producing problems. Although all marriages will have problems that cannot be anticipated, most serious problems are sufficiently common that we can usually prepare for them.

Here are some of the most common problems parents encounter:

1. Different and conflicting ideas about childrearing and discipline.
2. Conflict in roles as parents, spouses, and workers all at the same time.
3. Differing expectations by the wife and mother about how much time she devotes to the children and how much she devotes to her husband.
4. Difficulty in balancing personal needs with the needs of the family.
5. Maternal tendency to put the needs of the children above the emotional and sexual needs of her husband.
6. Difficulty in coming to grips with the magnitude of the parenting responsibility.
7. Under-appreciation of the degree of stress children place on a marriage and the degree that parenting is a one-way street of giving from parent to child.

Let's discuss each point.
Experience tells me that disagreements over childrearing

practices are at the heart of many husband-wife disputes. People seem to pretend that they will never have children or that the children will be perfect. Parenting methods should be a normal subject for engaged couples to discuss, but this does not seem to be the case.

Books on parenting should be read and discussed by the engaged couple, certainly by newly married couples, and issues should be settled well before the children are born. Decisions should be made on the whole issue of the wife-husband roles and their responsibilities. For example, how will they deal with the demands of the husband's job. Will the wife have to work and for how long? Will the husband's ego be threatened by his wife's work? Who will care for the children while both work? Who will decide how the extra money is spent? Should the wife quit work as soon as children are born? The list of topics is endless.

But the issue is preparation. Both sets of parents can help by asking the couple if they have thought about such things as discipline. If they have, what have they decided? Disagreements on this should be constructive, non-ego-threatening, and loving.

Five Basic Freedoms

Virginia Satir, a noted and experienced family therapist, says that as children we need to be given an "endowment" made up of five basic freedoms. Her thinking is that if these five freedoms are realized when we are children, we are allowed to enter adulthood as complete people, unburdened by the psychological baggage of our youth. If these five freedoms are not provided for children, incompleteness results, and we go through adulthood and parenthood still looking to others to meet these unmet needs from childhood. You and I may disagree on some of her wording, but the concept rings true.

Think with me for a moment about your own upbringing.

Remember how it felt to be a child in your family. Try to remember the good and bad times you had with your parents, the discipline, the gifts, illness and recovery. Think with me about what it was like to be the child you were and see if you can remember these five freedoms being functional for the children in your family, most especially *you!*

1. The freedom to see, hear, and perceive what is here and now, rather than what was, will be, or should be.

Children need to be able to experience their environment as it is at that moment. If Mom and Dad are too much into reminiscing about "the good old days" or groaning and complaining about how wicked and corrupt the world is, the children in that family can develop a truly perverted view of the world.

Some years back, while ministering in another area of the country, Linda and I became acquainted with another family in the same ministry. I did not use the term friend because the husband and father of the family "turned off" everybody with his *extreme* right wing, radical, conservative viewpoint on life. This poor fellow really thought that our government (under President Reagan, at the time) was already controlled by Communists and socialists and nothing, *absolutely nothing*, was going to persuade him otherwise.

Okay, everybody is welcome to his or her opinion, but this fellow would not let any conversation about anything culminate without trying to direct it to *his* concern, namely, the Communist takeover of the United States government. We could be talking about the Little League baseball game in progress, and he would want to talk about his pet theory of the "Commie" takeover. Buying a new car? Did I know that General Motors was a stooge of the Communist block? Would he like a soft drink? Okay, but did I know that this company was the major underwriter of left-wing politics in this country?

130

So he looks like a lunatic to others. Who cares?

His kids cared, that's who!

Three daughters and a baby son were going to be raised in this otherwise good Christian home, being exposed to such radical and totally unproven and unprovable ideas which probably scared them to death. These kids were not given the first freedom. That is, to perceive the world as it really is. Somehow this man's insecurity, even as a Christian, was soothed by his manic attitudes about the power of Communists in this country. Think of the burden he passed along to those four kids.

I really wonder about what he must be telling himself now that the Communist world is crumbling. I wonder if he realizes what his children, who are grown up now, probably think of him.

2. The freedom to think what one thinks, rather than what one should think.

The human brain is a wonder! Consisting of millions and millions of always-changing neurons, each carries the potential for creating an absolutely new thought, idea, or solution.

There may be nothing new under the sun, but it is not true of the brain's power to create. There are countless millions of absolutely new human thoughts every day. Some of these thoughts have taken us to the moon and back, cured polio, and become words for the poet's pen.

But some of us are really uncomfortable with creativity. Some of us were raised to be concerned about what we were thinking, told too often to "purify" our thoughts when we weren't thinking anything "impure" in the first place. Many of us were trained to be self-censors of creativity and now, as adults, we are hesitant at the opportunity to make a suggestion, remembering those early days when new thoughts meant bad thoughts.

Consider the creativity that was required of the disciples. Think of how revolutionary those "new" ideas and words being spoken by Jesus really were to those listening ears.

Were there conformists among that band of twelve who followed Jesus? Could a person be a conformist and still give his life for this new idea called Christianity?

No! There were no conformists following Jesus. His ideas were too radical for those Jewish men.

Ask yourself: Would my children feel the freedom to follow Jesus if they were in the places of those early Christians? Or have we taught them to "go along and get along" and stay away from new ideas?

I wonder!

The freedom to think is precious for our children and should not be frightened out of them.

3. The freedom to feel what one feels, rather than what one should *feel.*

There are, of course, feelings such as hatred and envy that we are to avoid at all costs. We recognize these. But too often we have a tendency to tell our children that "you shouldn't feel": (1) angry, (2) upset, (3) unhappy, (4) bored, (5) disappointed, (6) left out, and on and on. You can fill in the remainder based on your experiences with being told that you *shouldn't* feel the way you felt.

Feelings are most basic to smaller children and important to everyone. We have the ability to fool ourselves through our thoughts, but our feelings often give us away.

We need to legitimize our children's feelings, even though we may instruct them on how to deal with those feelings. No, the child should not feel jealous, but we can tell him that all children feel jealous sometimes and that God wants him to find a way *not* to feel jealous anymore. Jealousy is a sin, but we can tell him we will help him feel better about his

132

feelings of anger, jealousy, or being left out...and so will Jesus if we tell Him and ask Him to replace those feelings with ones that honor Jesus.

4. *The freedom to want and to choose what one wants, rather than what one* should *want.*

Again, as parents, we are in the correcting business with our kids. But we can still affirm the child's desires while helping her understand that what she desires (deceased puppy to come back to life) may not be within the realm of possibility or reasonable expectations.

But we do *not* say, "You should not want your puppy to live again," or "it's silly to want such a thing." These parental attitudes simply shame the child into believing that their desires are all silly and unworthy. What we want is *very* important to God our Father, and we should never ridicule our kids for wanting something we believe they cannot receive.

Can you handle another personal story?

Our youngest child, Jennifer, was just five years old when we moved from Detroit to Greenville, South Carolina. We had joined a Christian ministry there that did not pay very well, and though that was just fine with us because we knew that God had always and would always take care of His people, it was a little hard for the kids to understand that their parents did not have as much money for toys and such as when we lived and worked in Michigan.

But Jennifer was only five!

And Jennifer wanted a new bike, her first two-wheeler.

Jennifer and the other kids had been raised to believe that God answers prayer, but frankly, the Miller family had always been in a position financially to make sure that those, "I wish I had..." prayers were answered at birthday or Christmas time.

But we couldn't afford a new bike. Not just then.

133

We told Jennifer that the bike would have to wait until Christmas or her next birthday because we couldn't afford one for this birthday. She was not noticeably disappointed. She opened her birthday gifts and was happy and seemed to have as much fun as ever.

Later that same evening, our friends Dean and Mariann arrived for a planned visit from Michigan and told us that they had brought their daughter's bike with them because they thought that Jennifer could use it.

We woke Jennifer up and told her that Mr. and Mrs. Trondle had brought her a bike! We were more excited than she, much to our surprise. Jennifer got up and dressed, about ten p.m., went out on the porch, and practiced riding the bike.

When she came in, we were all amazed at how calm she was.

"Jennifer, aren't you surprised?"

"But, Daddy, I was *praying* for a bike. Wasn't it *supposed* to come?"

I still get chills every time I tell this story.

We must validate our children's wishes and encourage their faith even while helping to structure their thinking to be realistic. We don't know what God will do, and He seems to take great delight in pleasing children. Out of the mouths of babes comes truth!

  *5. The freedom from imposed role, the freedom to choose
   the kind of person one wants to become.*

Many who work with families in a helping-type relationship are concerned about the damage done by imposed roles for children. A role is what people expect of us in a given position.

A role says to us, "You are a firstborn son. Therefore, you must be _____." Or, "You are the eldest daughter and your mother is chronically ill. Therefore, you must_____."

Regardless of the specific role assignments, children put in this position are not allowed to develop their own God-given, unique talents, abilities, and personality characteristics. A child may become a "Little Parent" who is expected to take care of an ill or addicted Mom or Dad. Another may be required to be the "Mascot," responsible for cheering everyone up when things are bad. Still another might be expected to become a "Surrogate Spouse" and become involved in an incestuous relationship with her father when a mother has died or left the family. There are many other such roles: hero, scapegoat, star, victim, rescuer, caretaker, and family referee are just a few of these assigned and unwanted roles.

Children who experience these assigned roles will inevitably rise up to call their parents selfish, as they certainly are, but the damage done over the years of childhood and adolescence in one of the roles may take years and years to heal.

Is there hope?

Certainly! But once again, we rely on two things to effect a cure: one, the love and healing power of God, and second, parental awareness so that future damage is avoided.

As we have looked at these issues so far, remember our intent has been to raise issues for discussion and thought. This may be my family or yours we are looking at, or the family of a friend or relative, or a counselee, a church member. There are any number of possibilities. But awareness of the danger followed by adoption of God's principles for healing (confession, repentance, restitution, trust, forgiveness) can lead us out of the valley of bad parenting or even allow us to miss it altogether.

But we are not out of the valley yet, at least in principle. Now we need to turn our attention to five distinctly maladaptive family patterns and see what God has for us to learn there.

Five Family Patterns: The Family Hall of Shame

The following family patterns are known to be harmful to children and parents alike. They give us a point of reference by which we can examine our own families for traces of this toxin as well as opening doors to look at other families. From a practical point of view, the mere fact that you are reading this book indicates that your family will not be found among these five. But you and I have a ministry to perform with other families whenever the Lord so guides, and we are bound to come into contact with families such as these. Some will have recently become Christians and are trying faithfully to overcome many years of destructive family behavior. Others are just beginning to raise children and are trying to overcome some bad lessons learned from their own parents. What we are doing now is filling our ammunition belts for the battle for the family!

1. The dissolved or disrupted family.

The most common reason for the break-up of a family is the departure of the father. This may be precipitated by a separation or divorce, or he may simply have just abandoned the family. Children and teens feel a tremendous sense of rejection when this happens. Boys tend to become angry and rebellious, girls to become rebellious and hyper-mature, often becoming involved in sexual activity at an early age.

Most fathers, once divorced, are out of the picture completely within two years. If the family cannot re-group and find a structure for the family that will meet the needs of all the members, the family will almost certainly disintegrate totally and become nothing more than a place to eat and sleep for the kids, a damage factor that often continues well into adulthood.

A family can also be dissolved or disrupted involuntarily by the death or serious illness of one of the parents. Youngsters have an easier time under these circumstances, but the transition is still not easy. For the family to do the job

God intended, two parents are needed or one parent who can requisition strength from God to do the job of both parents.

2. The disturbed family.

This pattern is usually created by factors in the lives of the parents which are passed along to the children in the family. This may be a form of mental illness, family violence, intense verbal arguments, sexual abuse, enmeshment of parents in the lives of their children, or simply the child's exposure to poor parenting models. This may very well be a modern example of what the Bible means with regard to the sins of the fathers being passed along to following generations.

3. The abusive family.

There are four basic forms of child abuse: physical, sexual, emotional maltreatment, and neglect. Each of these tends to be generationally transmitted and each is a powerful, destructive force to the family. Most perpetrators of child abuse are family members and most are parents, a fact which obviously does great damage to the sense of safety and security so important to the psychological and spiritual well-being of any child.

There are many reasons for child abuse, but parents who see their children as "need suppliers" are far more likely to abuse their children than parents who see themselves as meeting the needs of their children. Children simply cannot do for adults what they should be getting from the Lord and other adults. The system will always collapse in the end, but not before major and life-changing damage has been done.

4. The inadequate family.

Some adults are unable to cope with the pressures and demands of everyday life. If these adults also happen to be parents, that inadequacy will be seen in their child-rearing as well. Some parents are socially, mentally, or physically handicapped and cannot meet the needs of their children. Others are addicted to drugs and/or alcohol, and the needs of their children come second to the demon inside them screaming for satisfaction. Still others are inadequate because they never learned to parent properly.

Inadequacy is the inability to meet the basic needs of the child as well as failing to guide his growth and development in a way that will enhance rather than limit his potential.

5. The anti-social family.

This family holds values not acceptable to most members of the society. The family may be criminal in its orientation, sexually exploitive of children, violent to outsiders, or cultic in its religious beliefs.

Anti-social families can be those who teach their children that it is all right to steal from outsiders or that family loyalty and secrecy are more important than the laws of the society in which they live, or that one's religion (not God's law) takes precedence over the laws and standards of society and even one's own family. We see the mafia, the Jonestown massacre, and other symptoms of this form of family dysfunction all around us.

Such deviant patterns were not created or desired by God, and they did not arise from nothingness. There was a cause, and that cause will almost certainly reflect forward into generation after generation unless consciously altered.

It takes a spiritual change of heart *plus* re-education in better parenting practices to make a real difference.

The next step is to go a bit farther in learning about good and bad families. I use the term "dysfunctional" to identify families in trouble simply because these can be good people wanting to do the right thing without knowing what the right thing is!

Characteristics for Comparison

A certain level of self-awareness is necessary for change. Compare your family environment with the following characteristics.

1. Communication among family members. Healthy

families are able to talk about almost anything with almost any family member. While some subjects may not be acceptable for everyone to hear, a general sense of openness pervades the family. Honesty is also found in the communication patterns of healthy families and seems to encourage a high degree of give and take among family members. Honesty, openness, clarity of message, and spontaneity are all common factors of the communication process in healthy families.

On the other hand, the communication patterns in less healthy, dysfunctional families tend to be vague rather than clear, evasive rather than honest, and non-reciprocal.

2. Relationships. Relationships among family members in healthy families are usually based on trust in each other, a desire to spend time with one another, a caring attitude, genuine warmth for other members of the family, shared responsibilities by all family members, and mutual satisfaction with the marriage by the spouses.

Dysfunctional families show a great deal of ambivalence in their feelings about the family. This ambivalence leads to a natural sense of distrust of each other; inconsistencies in dealing with problems and people, including the children, and anger developing into the most commonly expressed emotion in the family. The emotion most obviously missing in dysfunctional families is trust.

3. Emotions. Dysfunctional families are dominated by emotions of hopelessness, hostility, cynicism, and a certain degree of sadism. The key again is ambivalence, and this uncertainty normally leads to defensive postures when emotion-producing situations develop.

Healthy families have a much easier time dealing with emotions. There is love expressed, understanding that leads to genuine empathy when someone is having a problem, and general happiness. Along with these qualities, humor is present. A sense of humor seems totally missing in depressed

139

and mentally ill people, but it is always present in some amount in healthy people and healthy families.

4. Coping Ability. All families deal with stress; there is just no choice. Healthy families accept it as a normal, if unpleasant, part of life. They cope because of their ability to work with each other through the difficult situations, and a strong certainty that God is in control. Strength in numbers is the watchword of healthy families as they cope with problems.

Dysfunctional families are much more likely to attempt to avoid the situation or deny its severity. Coping in dysfunctional families is fantasy-based rather than reality-based, and this shows in the tendency to be disconcerted by situations and problems that are easily dealt with in other families.

5. Power Structure. In dysfunctional families, power is expressed in a hierarchical manner and is based on what many call a "pecking order." Often there are coalitions formed between children and one parent in order to get control away from the other parent. Discussion of choices is absent. Discipline tends to be rigid and authoritarian, reflecting the mindset and the personal insecurities of the parents.

Power is shared in healthy families because there is less to be lost in loaning out some parental power. Parents are more flexible and will listen to input from other members of the family. Decisions can be negotiated even though parents hold more power than the children. All viewpoints are considered and discussed. Discipline is present, but it is based more on authority and respect than power.

6. Role Differentiation. In healthy families, role boundaries are clear and well understood. The identity of each member is well defined and secure, and each is respected as an individual. Individuality and family membership are balanced so that neither is stifled.

In dysfunctional families, the boundaries are blurred,

leading to the kinds of problems previously mentioned. There tends to be a lot of blaming and scapegoating, mostly among the children. Everyone in the family seems to avoid taking responsibility for his or her own actions. It is in these families that we see some of the greatest long-term damage done to children.

How do you rate your family on these six variables?

I know that my family has changed dramatically through the years, and we are better at some of these qualities than we were in earlier years. As I think about it, I realize that it would be a pretty sad state of affairs if some improvements did not occur. We are supposed to become wiser as we age and gain experience.

Avoiding Parental Guilt

Some parents *ought* to feel guilty!

And if it takes feeling guilty to change a destructive family pattern, then guilt is worth it.

But most of us feel guilty when we should not because we place unreasonable and ungodly standards of perfection on ourselves and feel like failures because we are not *perfect* parents.

We can be good, godly parents without being perfect and without feeling guilty for our imperfections. We should know enough about *really* bad families to be able to see that we are doing a good job with our kids, one that pleases God.

Avoiding guilt in this sin-filled world means keeping our eyes continually on God and on His standards and expectations for us.

If we can do this, we should be able to keep guilt in its place and see the blessings of God in our family.

Points for Parents to Ponder

1. Do you identify with any of the elements in Catherine's story?

2. Do you, in any way, feel "stuck" at a level of development younger than your years?

3. Can you name two specific negative behaviors or attitudes that you inherited from your parents?

4. Did you answer "no" to more than one of the questions on family environment?

5. How would you diagnose your family health?

6. And family role division?

7. How about family emotional conditions?

8. And family structure?

9. Are you missing any of the "five freedoms" developed by Virginia Satir discussed in this chapter?

10. Would your family fit the description in the "Family Hall of Shame"?

("Yes" answers indicate tendency to accept the kind of parental guilt discussed in this chapter.)

9 / Single Parenting

Diane watched Jerry walk away. This time the divorce was final. There was no chance now that he would come back to them. She couldn't stop the tears. She didn't even try; she just didn't understand how she had any left.

She hadn't wanted the divorce. They had tried counseling. But nothing—not even the needs of his own children—could convince Jerry to drop his relationship with the other woman.

The months that followed were the most painful, angry, and desperate she had ever known. Her parents worried about her; she just couldn't get a hold on her emotions. She spewed over with tears, anger, and terror whenever she talked with them.

"How could he do this to me?" she raged. "How can I raise these two children alone?" she cried in terror.

The responsibility overwhelmed her, not just the financial burden. She'd carried the majority of that before the divorce. It was the burden of caring and providing training and emotional stability all by herself.

Her self-esteem hit zero and then dipped into the negative column.

She finally went for counseling, and it helped wash the anger and resentment against him away. She started to rebuild her self-image. She started to count her blessings, including her rewarding and well-paying job. But the loneliness, and the burden of the sole care of the children remained. It would take time, but somehow, some way she would make it.

I'm not going to bore you with divorce statistics. It is just about impossible to read a newspaper or listen to a news program without divorce and the changing status of the American family being mentioned at least once. We know plenty about divorce, but the problem is, we are still struggling as a church to find a way to deal with it!

But deal with it we must, and quickly, too! The problem has arrived at the church door. We are surrounded by Christian people suffering because their marriage partner has failed to honor their commitment to the marriage vows taken so seriously earlier. And those who work with children and teens know how devastating the break-up of the marriage can be.

We know how painful and slow a recovery can be, but recovery is critical—not only for the sake of our own lives and ministries, but also for the witness of the church.

Dealing with divorce in the church demands knowledge as well as compassion and empathy. Recovery requires knowledge and strength, and it is here that the church and the stressed Christian family must draw together. Hand-wringing, stone-throwing, and blame-tossing won't solve any problems. We must *deal* with the crisis in as Christian and humane a manner as possible. And what we do with this problem we must do quickly.

What are the needs of divorced Christian adults who are also parents? If Mother has custody, how can the church help? How can friends and family help? And what about Dad?

144

Whether he has custody of the children or just visitation rights, he is hurting, too!

Then there are the children, the always innocent victims of the decisions made by adults who decide to dissolve a marriage and a family. As parents, we divorce the children as well. No, we do not mean to, but the kids *feel* abandoned, deserted, isolated, incomplete, and strange after a family has dissolved.

Successful single parenting requires a great deal of extra effort and dedication from *both* parents at a time when Mom and Dad are probably absorbed in their own feelings of hurt and guilt. A tough job, this single parent assignment, but one that can be done for the glory of God and with a degree of success that may seem unimaginable.

Here's where we begin the process.

The World of the Single Parent

It's been said that only Christians shoot their wounded—and all too often it's true. In acknowledging the sin, we tend to shut off the flow of godly love toward the very needy people caught in divorce.

Too many of us surrender our accusatory attitudes only slowly, still questioning the innocence of the husband or wife who is forced to accept the decision of a spouse to end the marriage.

Why do we seem to want to find fault in these Christian men and women who truly did not seek to end their marriage? Why do we blame the victim in such sad cases?

We do so in order to protect ourselves and our own sense of marital security. We find fault so that we may delude ourselves into thinking that if *we* do not make those same suspected errors, this terrible thing will not happen to us.

False security to be sure.

Of course, there are no totally innocent husbands or wives. But there are countless divorces brought on by the behavior of just one of the partners, and it is this type of situation that most often presents itself to the church for recovery and healing.

Eleanor Kellogg had experienced such a trauma. Her insurance executive husband of twenty-two years had simply announced one day that God had "led" him into a relationship with another woman he now wished to marry, and even though *he* had no hard feelings toward his "neglectful" wife and the mother of their two children, their marriage was over.

Eleanor was devastated.

Was she a perfect wife? Of course not, but she was not the motivating force behind the divorce, no matter how hard her husband Bill tried to convince himself and others that she was the problem rather than his own sinful desires for another woman.

Bill proceeded with the divorce, ignoring all invitations for counseling and attempts at reconciliation offered by the counseling staff of their church. Bill had made up his mind, and the consequences of his decision kept me involved with this family for the next few years.

The Road to Guilt-Free Single Parenting

A famous Chinese proverb states, "A journey of a thousand miles begins with the first step," but I found it very difficult to convince Eleanor that her first step was, in fact, the beginning of her road to recovery and family health. As Eleanor and I began the counseling process, I was most interested and concerned with her attitudes about herself and her abilities as a parent.

Eleanor needed to know that one parent following God's principles for child-rearing can do a *better* job of parenting than *two* parents following their own wisdom and ignoring God. I needed to help this mother of two understand that her children needed *more* strength and structure from her now that Dad was no longer living in their home. And, I needed

146

to help her grasp the importance of controlling her own guilt so that she could raise her children properly *and* so she could recover her own self-esteem as a Christian woman.

Our journey was not going to be a thousand miles, but I knew from experience that that's what it looked like to Eleanor.

Problems of Single Parenting

The entire American social structure revolves around the two-parent system. Most of America still believes that the two-parent family is not only an ideal but also a reality.

In spite of a high and escalating divorce rate, the two-parent family *is* still the norm for America, a lifestyle practiced by *most* of us who are married and who have children.

But it is this very commonality that creates problems for single parents like Eleanor. School programs, church activities, community get-togethers all function under the assumption that the families involved are *mostly* two-parent families.

Letters come home from school addressed "to the parents of." Political and community mail-outs, even advertisements come addressed to "Mr. and Mrs. Consumer."

Over and over again Eleanor and thousands like her are reminded of how "different" they are and how they do not fit any longer with "normal" America. Add to this the tendency of some of us to "blame the victim," and it should be easy to see one major source of guilt after a marriage has ended.

Single parenting is also difficult and potentially guilt-producing because the wisdom of the family is lessened with the departure of one parent from the daily life of the family. Two heads are better than one, especially when there are children to raise. But one parent now bears most of the responsibility for healing the children's social and emotional wounds, taking care of homework, disciplining them when they need it, and doing all this in a spirit of love and acceptance at a time when *Mom* doesn't feel she is loved or accepted any longer.

In addition to being the only source of wisdom and advice for the family, every single parent eventually becomes exhausted with the double duty required. The single parents I know always seem to be very tired, a situation that can be expected to lessen their ability to deal with even normal family problems. This burden may even lead to physical or psychological problems.

Other concerns of the Christian single parent include sex-role development for boys raised by a mother or girls raised by a father. More than 90% of children live with Mother following a break-up. Boys without a father in their lives on a regular basis *may* experience some problems in finding their identity as a male. Girls are more at risk for a too-young marriage or an unwed pregnancy because of the emotional reaction that she, too, has been rejected as a female by Dad's departure.

Boys seem to suffer more than girls in other areas as well. Mother-raised boys are more at risk for delinquency and school-related problems including truancy and poor academic performance. Boys, and to a lesser extent girls, are more likely to become involved with alcohol and drugs during adolescence, become sexually active, drop out of high school, and are even more likely to consider suicide compared to kids whose parents are still together.

Is there a reason for single-parent guilt?

Absolutely!

Virtually *every* problem is more common in father-absent children.

Both girls and boys raised by a single parent are more likely to experience school phobia, usually from grades four to seven, and the trauma is usually more severe in girls. School somehow becomes a negative stimulus for many divorced children and actually changes from being a pleasant place for elementary children to being one of discomfort and pain.

Along with the school phobia, many children worry excessively about the possible death of their remaining parent. I have known several children and teenagers who made phone calls to the parent's place of employment or entertainment to make sure they had arrived safely. This clearly stems from the fact that children in divorced families are less secure than others. Naturally they worry about their remaining source of security.

Child care is a common problem in divorced families. Making arrangements for the pre- and after school hours as well as preschool and summer care is often at the top of the list of problems faced by a divorced parent. A lot of confusion as well as a lack of knowledge concerning the choice of good care is predominant. This, in turn, produces guilt because the need for child care is so crucial, especially for mothers.

On top of all the concern for quality care, the parent is then plagued with the financial burden the care produces and guilt because she cannot be with the child.

Single parents don't need to be told that they have difficult problems to face. But other Christians can help by being aware of the special needs of the single parent families in our churches.

Single Parent Styles

Being the sole parent in the home demands certain kinds of adjustments. Some of the adaptations are good and some are not. Whether they are good or bad, the following examples illustrate the needs of single-parent families.

Most noticeable of the changes is the change to sole executive of the family. Sometimes single parents call on relatives or outsiders to substitute for them. Whether they are grandparents, older brothers and sisters, or a live-in housekeeper, they are all mother/father surrogates. They can be very helpful on a temporary basis, but they rarely last.

Then there is the parent who has surrendered to the pressures of the situation and quit being a parent. These "pseudo parents" no longer have control over their children; in reaction, they may even behave as one of the children.

The negative impact of divorce can be reduced for children and adolescents. Reduced, not eliminated. One of the many tragedies of divorce today is that there will always be some amount of hurt to family members not directly involved in the marital disruption. In a survey of college students in reference to their memories of growing up, researchers found that the parents' divorce was remembered almost unanimously as the single *worst* thing these young people had experienced.

There are tactics to reduce the side effects of divorce, but reducing the pain is different from preventing the pain. Once the divorce has occurred, the pain usually lasts for a lifetime.

But this doesn't mean the guilt *must* occur or that the damage of a divorce *must* produce very negative results in children or teens.

This is where parental guilt becomes an important issue. If Mom and Dad really are willing to put the needs of the children above their own following a divorce, youngsters can be enabled to deal with what has happened. Children are usually resilient when family crises occur, often much more so than parents and other adults. Kids just do not seem to retain the negatives of what has happened *unless* the two most important people in their lives behave in ways that encourage the problem.

What do parents do that would create such long-term damage? What do we adults do when a marriage ends that would create guilt in us and pain in our children? Consider the following.

150

Guilt-Producing Mistakes

Mistake #1. Assume that the children are not able to understand what has happened to their family and so must be kept "ignorant" of what has taken place and why.

No greater mistake is possible for a divorcing couple than to refuse to tell the kids, in an age-appropriate way, what is going on. Not only will the youngsters in the family deeply resent the lack of trust and confidence in their ability to understand, but parents will eventually feel even more guilty and become less able to lead the family well.

Mistake #2. Don't tell the children what will be happening in the days or weeks to come.

It is the uncertainty of what this separation and divorce means that threatens the security of the children and leads to outbursts of bad behavior, parental over-reaction, and resultant guilt for the parent. Let the children in on the changes that will be necessary and then enlist them to help with the transitions. Keeping them in the dark is not only guilt-producing for parents but tends to prolong the readjustment and recovery period.

Mistake #3. Tell children and teens all the "nasty" details so they will be on your side and against your spouse.

Kids need to see both parents as heroes. Though negative information may be factually correct at the time, it is *never* appropriate to share details. There may come a day when, as adults, you can share what really happened, but to do this with youngsters will only compound their pain and increase your guilt over having told them. The Bible tells us to speak the truth in love, and though the details may be true, we do not show genuine love and concern for our kids when we burden them with unnecessary details about the failure of one of their parents.

*Mistake #4. Keep the divorce a secret from the kids'
teachers, other school personnel, and Sunday School
workers.*

Guilt and shame are common emotions in both parents
and children following a marital break-up, and it is natural
to want to keep as much of it secret for as long as possible.
But when it comes to teachers and counselors, they *need* to
know what has been happening at home so they can be
understanding and supportive in the recovery process when
the child reacts negatively. Keeping this a secret is the natural
thing to do, but it is as unwise as it is natural.

*Mistake #5. Use the kids to carry negative messages between
hostile parents.*

Divorced parents can absolutely insure their own guilt
and the increased insecurity and acting-out of their children
by assassinating their heroes. The criticisms may be true, the
questions may be legitimate, but children must never be
recruited into either Mom's army or Dad's. Being told to
"ask your father where the support payment is when
you see him this weekend" simply destroys any opportunity
the child or teen may have for healthy adjustment. Similar
messages in return of "tell your mother she'll get the
check when I get paid" is no better. Preserve their heroes at
all costs.

*Mistake #6. Use the children as couselors for your prob-
lems.*

As tempting as this may be, and as invited as it may be at
times, children and teens must never be allowed to become
"burden bearers" for Mom's or Dad's troubles. The giving-
receiving pattern in a healthy family is always and only a
one-way street leading *from* parents *to* the kids.

This seems to be especially likely when Mom has daughters
who are pre-teen or teenage and who really seem to want to

help Mom feel better. Though well intentioned, this inevitably produces negative results through the unavoidable loss of confidence in Mom's ability to help the youngsters deal with their difficulties. How can a mother or father who is suffering and struggling with personal problems help the kids with theirs? Of course they cannot, and the eventual loss of confidence can be far more destructive than any temporary good. Immature minds cannot comprehend what parents are going through no matter how much they want to help.

Mistake #7. Make promises and then fail to keep them.

Security is always the key issue in children's ability to adjust to family changes in a healthy manner, and security is built on parental behavior almost exclusively.

Promises should be made carefully and then fulfilled with great care, especially in the months following the departure of one parent from the home. Promises kept are security builders and promises unfulfilled, even for good reason, create great and long-lasting problems in parent trust.

Mistake #8. Be extra lenient after the divorce because you feel a little guilty.

The average parent becomes lenient after a divorce because of the need *of the parent* to "make it up" to the kids. In spite of knowing that children and teens need *more* structure after a divorce, parents seek to soften their own guilt feelings by "easing up" on matters of discipline.

The unfortunate result of this leniency is that the children feel more threatened, and tend to act out and misbehave just to see if they can pressure Mom or Dad into "proving" that they are still in control. This reluctance on the part of the parents to provide structure results in more discipline problems, more parental guilt because they feel like poor parents, then more leniency, and the cycle continues.

Mistake #9. Assume that your children know you love them and will continue to care for them.

I can remember fathers of my parents' generation proclaiming, "I don't need to tell the kids I love them. I come home with a paycheck, don't I?" We adults sometimes overlook a child's need to be reminded verbally that he is loved and will continue to be cared for under any circumstances.

Particularly after a marital disruption, kids need constant reminders not only that they are still loved but also that they had no role in the decision to dissolve the marriage and, therefore, have no power to "heal" the broken family. Our problem is that we think like the adults we are and forget that the child's mind needs some reassurances that we may take for granted. When in doubt, give them anyway!

Mistake #10. Be so absorbed with your own feelings that you have no time to listen to the thoughts and feelings of the kids.

The church needs to provide burden-bearers for a mother and/or father who has gone through a divorce. This is important in order to protect the kids from becoming submerged in parental emotions and without an opportunity to express their own. We need to remind ourselves that the kids still need to have someone to listen to them and support them in their feelings. A parent who is unable to do this will experience extreme guilt later and will probably be unable to find a way to make it right with the kids.

Appropriating the Mind of God

The image children have of themselves is what they see reflected in the eyes of their parents. Mom or Dad cannot let their feelings of failure or sorrow cause them to close their eyes to the needs of their children. If the kids see Mom or Dad constantly depressed, they will assume that is what they

154

are to feel, too. And if they see Mom or Dad as emotionally needy, they will try to meet those emotional needs at the expense of their own.

And, if they see in Mom's or Dad's eyes the need for a scapegoat, one of the kids will become that scapegoat. If another sees the need for a perfect child, then one will try to become perfect. Another may see a need for a bad child so that Mom or Dad can use them as a target instead of each other, and one will become that bad child.

Our kids will fill the roles they see as needed in our eyes.

Remember Bill and Eleanor Kellogg, the couple I mentioned earlier? Eleanor was able to find a "burden bearer" in her church, a counselor who could share with her the things we have been looking at and one with whom Eleanor could express her feelings while protecting her children. Eleanor has been able to do a good job of being a single parent primarily because she was helped to put aside her guilt feelings and be the strong parent her children needed.

But Bill Kellogg, that's another story. I still see Bill once in a while, and I have been told by a reliable source that the relationship that caused his marriage to dissolve has itself dissolved. Bill has started to drink. He feels like a failure partly because he *has* failed and partly because he has no one with whom to share his feelings of guilt. It is usually harder for dads to get help, mostly I guess, because of all the "macho" stuff promoted in our culture.

Bill has not learned what Eleanor has learned—that there is a God of forgiveness who will wipe away all our guilt if we will but ask. But right now, Bill cannot forgive himself for the decision he made that cost him his family.

God wants us to keep our families intact for His glory and the well-being of the children He has given us to raise for Him.

I am not at all convinced that guilt-free single parenting is a reasonable expectation. Even in the situations cited above, the apparently innocent partners are inevitably going to feel guilty about the break up of the marriage no matter how obvious the shortcomings of the other partner.

Our hope is to diminish the guilt of the innocent party *and* the children in order to help them cope with what is left of their former lives and to build toward the new.

Several facts illustrate the stress these families experience. Divorced people are significantly more at risk for automobile accidents, suicide, and homicide. Fatal illnesses, especially cancer and heart disease, are much more likely for the divorced. Admission rates to psychiatric hospitals are about nine times higher for the divorced than the married. All these negatives can be linked to intense guilt over the divorce and an inability to find ways to resolve the pain. And for those involved in children's ministries, it is absolutely vital to remember that divorce is just about the worst thing that can happen in the life of a child.

It is up to the church, the body of Christ on earth, to minister to those hurting from divorce, to understand the guilt, and to administer compassion.

Points for Parents to Ponder

1. Are you a single parent?

2. Are you at risk for separation or divorce?

3. Are your parents or in-laws divorced?

4. Is the fear of being abandoned by your spouse real for you?

5. Do you often feel that your children are unconcerned about how you feel?

6. How about your spouse?

7. Have you broken a promise to one of the kids in the last thirty days?

8. Do you feel that you are too lenient with the kids?

9. Can you identify in any way with Bill or Eleanor Kellogg?

10. Does parenting seem a never-ending or burdensome task?

("Yes" answers indicate tendency to accept the kind of parental guilt discussed in this chapter.)

10 / Legalism and Parent Guilt

There are two great perils facing the Christian family heading into the twenty-first century. The first and oldest peril is liberalism. Since the days of the gnostics in the first centuries, fallen men have sought a way to make Christ's message more palatable, more appetizing to the masses hungry for a polite answer to the sin-sickness that threatens to overwhelm them. Liberalism tries to weaken the message of repentance and salvation to give the illusion that Jesus really meant to include everyone no matter what they believed about the gospel message.

Liberalism we recognize!

It is an old enemy, even a "comfortable" enemy because we believe liberals distinguish themselves by their attitudes and behavior and in so doing, make themselves easy targets for our sermons, books, and fears.

Liberalism has taken on new names today, things like New Age philosophy, a unity-oriented religion seeking to "release" the "god" who lives within us. Even some of the better known television evangelists preach new-ageisms by asking their audience to see themselves as "little gods," seemingly oblivious to Satan's glee and traps. Denominations, ignoring God's clearly spoken Word, admit women and homosexuals to the clergy.

Liberalism will always be a problem for Bible-believing Christians, but we tend to believe we can recognize it and deal with it.

But legalism is another mater. It is just as common and ancient as liberalism, but it is capable of causing much greater damage to the Christian family because many of "us" willingly embrace its dogma.

Just as liberalism is a comfortable enemy, legalism is often a comfortable friend, a mindset and spiritual orientation that lulls us into complacency and arrogant smugness, causing us to feel secure behind our isolationist barricades, confident that Jesus will return for our little group first.

Liberalism on the left. Legalism on the right. Biblical Christianity in the middle.

The Christian Family and Legalism

The atmosphere in the room was reflected in Harold Franks' face. His frown was accentuated by the rising flush on his face as he clenched and unclenched his fists.

"She did what?" he thundered.

Mary Franks stood by, as indignant as her husband. She had only learned the news that afternoon at her weekly Bible study. Rose Foster was always quick to carry tales, and her son had seen Sally leaving the theater.

"She went to the movie Saturday night instead of going to Judy's," the girl's mother confessed.

Harold turned on his daughter. "How many times have we discussed movies and things like that. You know they are worldly. You know that Christians don't do those things.

Besides that you lied to us! You said you were going to Judy's."

"I did go to Judy's—first," Sally countered, determined to stand up to her uncompromising parents. "Daddy, I'm seventeen years old. I'm a senior in high school. Why don't you trust me?"

"That should be obvious enough, young lady. I've just told you, you lied to us!"

"Only because you made me," she challenged.

"I made you?" Harold's blood vessels stood out as he yelled at his daughter.

"Yes! I can never talk to you. You never will listen to what I think about some things. I love Jesus, and I love you and Mom, but..."

"But nothing. You are our daughter, and you will do what you are told as long as you live in this house. Do you understand me? Going to that trash downtown!"

She tried to interrupt, "It wasn't trash!"

"Don't you interrupt me, young lady. I can't believe you would deliberately humiliate your mother and me like that. After all we've done. After all we've taught you. You shape up, young lady, or else."

"Or else what, Daddy? Are you going to throw me out on the streets?" She continued to challenge them although her voice trembled and she held her hands together so they wouldn't shake so much.

Her father was reacting, too, fighting to find a way out of the corner into which he had painted himself. Throw her out? How could he do that? But if he backed down now, where would that leave him? He swallowed his questions and delivered a typical authoritarian parental reply: "If that's what you make me do!"

Sally couldn't take any more. She was certain now that they didn't love her. She knew they'd never change, that she'd never be able to talk to them. The tears finally ran down her cheeks. She pressed her fist to her mouth, turned, and fled the room.

Legalism is one of those "buzz" words like abortion and homosexuality which allow no room for fence sitters. Legalist parents raise their children in the philosophy of Christian parenting taught to them as they grew up. However, increasingly, that framework of legalism produces a tremendous guilt in parents when the children and teenagers don't comply.

I hope you will stay with me for this chapter while I talk very much parent to parent.

Our focus is on guilt as a controlling element in Christian parenting, but the question may arise as to the relevance of legalism. Is it *really* a problem for Christian families? What does legalism have to do with parental guilt?

One thing I have learned in the thirty years I have been a Christian and the almost twenty-five years I have been a parent is that legalism hurts families.

Period!

Eventually, *every* family functioning from a legalistic perspective suffers for its legalistic attitude. What's more, that suffering will be passed from generation to generation because children learn their parenting skills and attitudes from their parents.

Legalism does not preclude love and sound doctrine, but it may make the practice of those doctrinal beliefs and the expression of that love more difficult at times. Absolute values based on the Bible are one thing. Absolute values created by man, based on personal preference, are something else entirely. And the authoritarian/absolutism mindset of legalism doesn't encourage the attitude of searching the Scriptures daily on a personal basis.

Parents under this kind of pressure are likely to produce children who either rebel in adolescence or become church mice with no opinions of their own, no thoughts of their own.

Only what comes from parent or pastor is considered. No decisions are made on their own through personal conviction and personal study of God's Word.

Legalism adds one's personal preferences or interpretations to God's Word. Most legalists teach that while salvation is by grace alone, it can be *measured* or *evaluated* or *judged* by one's appearance, behavior, associations, music preferences, hair length or style, and on and on. We become not only "others-critical" but "self-critical." We not only expect "others" to feel guilty for their behavior but we also expect that we will feel guilty for ours as well.

Legalism teaches that what a person truly is is what they look like, act like, and who their friends are.

Yes, I believe that externals often indicate what groups the adolescent aspires to please. A Christian teenager who wants to punk her hair to a bright purple and wear fluorescent clothing has a problem. But the problem is not necessarily one of salvation as much as it is a lack of Christian maturity and understanding of what the Bible says about personal testimony.

The parent who misreads the adolescent and reacts legalistically can do irreparable damage to that teenager's relationships to her family and to her God.

Legalism hurts families!

Always, eventually.

Legalism teaches that guilt is a natural and desirable state of spirit.

Feelings of guilt that move us closer to repentance of sin and closeness to God are good. But legalistic guilt tends to communicate a "worm of the earth" mentality that will give any child difficulty. Children are in the process of developing self-concept, and a judgmental, exclusionary home can develop self-righteousness on one hand or a sense of hopelessness on the other. Raising our children in such an environment teaches them to judge more than to love.

Families are the "home base" of love and nurture as well as admonition for our children. But legalism "qualifies" that love with conditions rather than the unconditional variety that God teaches in His Word. This love defies rational explanation. It's the love Paul wrote about in Ephesians 3:19, "And to know the love of Christ, which passeth knowledge, that ye might be filled with all the fulness of God."

The question we must ask is, "What would Jesus do?" Then we must remember this is the Jesus who ate with sinners, cared personally for ungrateful lepers by touching them, refused to condemn the woman taken in adultery, and enabled a thief to enter heaven on the day He was crucified.

Guilt based on legalism chases us away from God rather than toward Him and the forgiveness He offers. Guilt growing out of legalistic parenting teaches that God is at least as harsh and critical as our parents. What picture of our heavenly Father do we portray to our children?

One thing is for sure, Jesus was not a legalist. Jesus would talk to anyone, walk with anyone, offer salvation to anyone who would listen. Do you feel about people the way Jesus felt about people? Are your kids free to love others who are different?

Guilt is created in parents when they believe their success as parents depends on the behavior of their children. Guilt is created when they accept responsibility for the actions of other human beings who happen to be their children.

But Christian parents should only feel guilty when they consciously do something that harms their children in some way and fail to correct the error. They should *not* feel guilty when they have studied the Bible, prayed, and are doing what they know to be right.

Rules and Legalism

So, is it possible for a guilt-free parent to believe in rules? Certainly. Without rules, children feel insecure and unloved.

163

Rules in a Christian family are an encouragement to spiritual growth, but they should not be our *measure of spiritual growth.*

Rules in the family are not the destination but the road map!

Rules for children and teenagers are like the white lines painted along the *edges* of the highway to keep drivers from wandering off into the ditches on either side.

Christian parents can believe in the value of rules and hold strong, godly personal convictions without losing their balance and falling into legalism. They can, if they keep reminding themselves that rules are the means to the end and not the end in themselves. My goal as a Christian parent should not be to have grown children who are good rule-obeyers. It should be to have children who *want* to live a disciplined Christian life and understand why.

Points for Parents to Ponder

1. Do you accept the preferences of authority figures as long as they claim it is part of Bible doctrine?

2. Do you recognize an "us–them" aspect to your life as a Christian?

3. Do you believe obedience is the greatest virtue for a Christian?

4. Are you more self-critical after attending church than before?

5. Do you believe a Christian can be "disowned" by bad behavior?

6. Would you change churches if you could? Would your children? Why?

7. Have legalistic attitudes created unrealistic self-expectancies in your children or teenagers that may be stifling their personal contentment in the Lord?

8. Do you (and your church) encourage a personal study of God's Word and open discussion of personal convictions?

9. Have you reacted as Mary or Harold Franks?

10. Can you identify the buzzwords you have used to pigeonhole people?

("Yes" answers indicate tendency to accept the kind of parental guilt discussed in this chapter.)

11 / The End of Guilt

What God Wants Parents to Know

The mind of God is revealed in His Word, and the Holy Spirit leads parents in ways which do not contradict that Word. But the Word speaks in two ways: in global generalities and in matters of great specificity.

God's message to parents falls in the general category.

He has not left specific instruction on the subject of child raising because He knows human nature too well. He knows Christians would make idols of those *methods*, and forget about the inner person which concerns Him the most.

It is that inner person with whom all parents must first concern themselves, too. We must see our lives transformed by the renewing of our minds (Romans 12:1-2) so we can become the kind of person God wants us to be from the inside out. When we follow that precept, all other aspects of our lives will fall into place—including the rearing of our children. That doesn't mean that our methods will be flawless or our paths free of stumblingblocks. It does mean that we will be given the insight we need to bring our children to the place where they can make a willing and positive decision for God—if that is what they choose to do.

This wisdom of God allows parents to develop in their individual lives while they raise their children without focusing on the secondary issue of methods.

We need to remember that God wants us to be the best parents *we* can be, not the best parents *anyone* can be. We can please God by being "good-enough" parents. We do not need to feel guilty because we have proven to be as imperfect in our parenting as we are in all other things.

The good-enough parent!

Interesting concept, isn't it?

And if we are to see ourselves as imperfect but still pleasing to God in spite of these imperfections, the next step will be to forgive ourselves for the real or imagined errors we make as parents.

The question is not whether we can forgive "others" for less than our best parenting, but whether we can forgive *ourselves* for those parenting experiences.

The Bible gives us many examples of people forgiving others. Esau forgave Jacob; Joseph forgave his brothers; David forgave Saul; Solomon forgave Adonijah, and Jesus forgave His enemies

But can *you* forgive yourself?

You must. This is the *only* way you will be able to get back to being a fully functioning Christian parent again. If you are currently raising children or teenagers, your ability to parent effectively will continue to be limited by your lack of self-forgiveness.

Just do it! Say it right outloud!

"I am a good-enough parent!"

"God doesn't expect me to be perfect."

"God loves me in spite of the mistakes I *will* make with my children or teens."

The guilty-parent syndrome doesn't have to control your life. Not anymore!

God doesn't hold us responsible when our children make the wrong choices or choose the wrong path after we have tried our best under God to follow biblical principles and raise that child to godly living.

The guilt Christian parents usually feel is not from God. Even if wrong methods have been used, sin committed, or biblical principles ignored, a repentant parent should be relieved of guilt. There must be repentance and commitment to change, of course, but there shouldn't be guilt.

In the years I have worked with parents in family counseling situations, *most* have shared feelings of guilt with me. They almost always ask the same question: "What did we do wrong?"

The answer—probably very little.

Parents can do more damage to their families with false guilt than any damage done by children who are disobedient and/or misbehaving. In fact, parents can shorten their own lives and stunt the work of God in their lives if they hold on to intense and unrelieved guilt.

It is simply *impossible* for one human being to control totally the behavior of another human being—even a child. If the child *wants* to do wrong, there is virtually nothing a parent can do to stop that behavior. They can try motivation to divert the child; they can certainly pray, but sometimes the child or teenager is so determined to try something and so resistant to any suggestions that the pleas of parents *and* the voice of the Holy Spirit are ignored.

When Linda and I came to the conclusion that—short of God's intervention we were helpless to control our children's choices—then things began to change for the better in our family. It wasn't that we were hopelessly helpless but that we gained the simple awareness that God has to work things out in each life, parent or child.

Children of believers are extremely likely to turn out just as their parents want them to. Parents are the single most influential factor in shaping a child's character, values, goals, life-direction. Eighteen or more years of living with one set of Christian parents will, in the long run, overwhelm any other temporary influence—friends, school, or anything else. Your children will turn out much like their parents, and probably better.

The children of big shots and little shots alike get into trouble sometimes, but they get through it and over it! Nobody's perfect. However, parents may not get over the misbehavior as quickly as their children because parents suffer more pain and embarrassment than children and for a longer period. The truth is—parents shouldn't.

God *is* in control of Christian families. Parents are the custodians of their children, loaned to them for a while. They *facilitate* God's work in the lives of their children, but they do not *do* the work of God in them.

All parents are in this together, even when they feel the most alone. There is not only nothing new under the sun, there is also no sin common to one child that is not common to all children.

Parents lose a great deal when they have no opportunities to discuss their children in order to compare not only what works but also what doesn't work with other parents. So if nothing else, find some other parents with whom you can share ideas, trials, successes, failures. One of the greatest gifts parents can give each other comes from parents listening to other parents. There is comfort in knowing that other parents have already experienced and survived situations you are enduring. What's more comforting is to learn that most of those children turned out just fine. A third comfort is the fact that not only is there light at the end of the tunnel but also that the tunnel is a whole lot shorter than it looks.

What Parents Want Their Children to Know

Parents need to let their children know that they are no longer willing to accept responsibility for their behavior. Children must get the message that their parents recognize the fact that they cannot stop them completely from doing wrong. So, if the child *chooses* to do wrong, he or she will have to pay the price, not the parents. This is true parent power because it is a state of mind, not of muscle.

The state of mind that gives parents this power is influence rather than actual physical control. It is the lifestyle and testimony of the parents, not necessarily the paddle. We must let our children know that while we will do everything possible to make it difficult for them to do wrong and everything possible to make it easy for them to do right, the choice is ultimately theirs.

We must also teach our children that they answer to God, not just to us when they do wrong. They must know that we act as God's representatives as we lead our families. This requires us to deal with the children as we believe God wants us to. Ultimately, we both answer to God.

When we let our children know that they are *loaned* to us for a little while but that they belong to God for eternity, we show them that we, too, have a higher accountability. We must teach our children that they can escape our influence and control, but they cannot hide from God.

Then we need to let our children know that our love does not relieve the children themselves of their accountability to parents and to God. Our children need a clear understanding that obeying God is not slavery but free choice that will open doors to a rich life full of meaning, but it is a choice each person must make.

And to cement the family relationship, we need to let our children know that there are only two relationships that supersede our relationship as parent and child: our personal relationship to God and our relationship to our spouse.

170

The End of Guilt

One last word: Take it easy on yourself. The fact that you have taken time to read this book means that you are probably sufficiently concerned about parenting skills; you are probably doing a good job.

If you have read it because you have a specific concern and this book has confirmed that you have a problem, get the help that you need so that you can enjoy your children now as well as throughout their adult years.

If we were face to face right now, I would tell you that if you are like the great majority of Christian parents with whom I talk, I am very sure that you are doing a good job with your children, even though they may turn strange on you sometimes.

This too shall pass. If you don't insist on punishing yourself for the behavior of others, you will have a lifetime of love and fellowship with your children.

No. You're not a perfect parent. But the good news is— you don't have to be!

God bless you as you move ahead into a new realm of effective, guilt-free parenting.

60774

Help! I'm not a perfect parent overcomin
248.845 M647h   60774

Miller, David R.
Overton Memorial Library